THE DIMENSIONS OF PRIVACY

GARLAND REFERENCE LIBRARY
OF SOCIAL SCIENCE
(VOL. 98)

THE DIMENSIONS OF PRIVACY
A National Opinion Research Survey
of Attitudes Toward Privacy

Conducted by
Louis Harris & Associates, Inc.
and
Dr. Alan F. Westin
Professor, Public Law and Government,
Columbia University

GARLAND PUBLISHING, INC. • NEW YORK & LONDON
1981

Library of Congress Cataloging in Publication Data

Main entry under title:

The Dimensions of privacy.

  (Garland reference library of social science; v. 98)
    1. Privacy, Right of—United States—Public opinion.
2. Public opinion—United States. I. Westin, Alan F.
II. Louis Harris and Associates. III. Series.
JC596.2.U5D55   323.44'8'0973   80-9010
ISBN 0-8240-9372-0   AACR2

Printed on acid-free, 250-year-life paper
Manufactured in the United States of America

Contents

THE DIMENSIONS OF PRIVACY

Conceptual Framework

Public concern about privacy—more specifically, the potential abuse or misuse of personal information by business and by government—has increased steadily throughout the Seventies as documented in previous Harris surveys.

This trend has stemmed largely from the increasingly technological, computer-oriented nature of our society in which countless determinations, ranging from credit, insurance and job promotions to Social Security disbursements to Census-based allocations of public funds, are now based on the collection of so-called "personal data."

*Today, it is virtually impossible to own a home, drive a car, **obtain a loan,** enter a hospital or apply for any kind of financial assistance without relinquishment of some personal information.*

Concern about the relinquishment of such information, however, has not been solely a trend of the Seventies for it was in the prior decade that alarms were sounded from many quarters about the then emerging phenomena of "data processing," "data banks" and that catch-all, "surveillance."

In particular, fears mounted in the Sixties about how the then new computer-based technologies might outpace the traditional norms by which Americans had come to live with respect to their expectations of personal privacy, to public disclosure and to even "limited" surveillance.

By the early 1970s, growing public concern about the perceived erosion of privacy prompted a number of studies, most of which were conducted to assess how the new technologies of data processing and surveillance were actually developing.

By the mid-1970s, the first wave of new responses to the then officially labelled "privacy problem" surfaced, taking the form of federal and state laws as well as new privacy policies promulgated by some of the more progressive, generally larger corporations.

Today, five years after passage of the 1974 Federal Privacy Protection Act and three years after its "offspring," the Privacy Protection Study Commission, was spawned, a number of fundamental concerns about privacy confront government and business policymakers:

- *How much headway has actually been made in safeguarding the privacy of Americans—have we basically "solved" the privacy issue?*

- *Or have we failed to solve the privacy issue—have we, in fact, made a few, or several, serious misjudgments about privacy . . . mistakes which must be redressed with new voluntary and legal policies?*

- *Have we sufficiently considered a variety of privacy "choices" which might be available in the light of ever-evolving technological, organizational and social change?*

- *Are there better ways to put the individual—as consumer, social service client, employee, patient, advocate—in a position of greater control over his or her personal information?*

It is within the context of these broad questions—each of which could easily be the foundation of separate surveys or studies—that the specific focus of this survey was determined: namely, to learn to what degree privacy can and should be

3

Privacy

protected in an intensely service-oriented, technologically-based society—a society whose collective "marketplace" is fundamentally fueled by the collection, storage and use of the personal information of its citizens.

Accordingly, five general areas were singled out for exploration:
- **The personal dimensions of privacy**—how Americans, as individuals, perceive privacy today and the degree to which they feel their privacy has been eroded in recent years.
- **The employee/employer relationship**—how Americans assess their privacy at work, what they feel their employer does not have a right to know about them, what "privacy rights" they feel they should have in the workplace, what measures they feel employers should take to better safeguard their privacy.
- **The privacy-intensive industries**—how Americans view the degree to which industries such as insurance, credit, medical, computer, etc. have invaded their privacy.
- **Government and privacy**—how Americans feel about the way federal, state and local government agencies collect and use personal information about individuals.
- **How to protect privacy**—what does the public want protected by law and by private enterprise to insure a fair balance between the desire for privacy and the need for personal information to obtain various services and benefits.

Survey Sample

Given the scope of these five broad areas, it was felt that the survey sample should be equally broad. Accordingly, a total of 2,131 interviews—all of which were in person, with each interview lasting approximately an hour—were conducted.

Specifically, the sample included:
- **The adult American population**—a representative cross-section of 1,513 American adults were interviewed between November 30 and December 10, 1978.
- **Selected "leadership groups"**—a total of 618 representatives from 10 selected groups were interviewed between November 27, 1978 and January 4, 1979.

The "leadership" sample was comprised of the following:

Public sector representatives
- 77 Congressmen (or their aides) who have been involved with privacy legislation
- 53 Federal regulatory officials involved with privacy-related regulation, activity, etc.
- 42 law enforcement officials
- 33 state insurance commissioners

Private sector representatives
- 200 business employers, including corporate personnel officers
- 36 computer industry executives
- 36 life insurance and non-life insurance executives
- 40 major credit card company executives (including large retailers and major oil companies which distribute credit cards)
- 32 credit industry executives (including representatives from insurance companies, savings banks, and savings and loan associations)
- 36 commercial bank executives

Further details about the methodology used in this survey are described in the technical appendix to this report.

Study Highlights

*This section identifies the major findings of **The Dimensions of Privacy.***

The section does not include much of the data relating to the leadership groups surveyed or the finer shadings of interpretation, as such material may be found in each of the chapters which follow this section of key findings.

The Personal Dimensions of Privacy

Public Concern with Threats to Personal Privacy

- *The American people are greatly concerned about threats to their personal privacy. This concern is pervasive throughout society. Public concern about threats to personal privacy has jumped 17 percentage points in the past year—from 47% in January 1978 to 64% in December 1978.*

The "Right to Privacy"

- *3 out of 4 Americans now believe the "right to privacy" should be akin to the inalienable American right to life, liberty and the pursuit of happiness.*

Privacy and "The 1984 Syndrome"

- *One out of every three Americans believe that our society is very close to or already like the type of society described by George Orwell in his book **1984**, a society in which "virtually all personal privacy had been lost and the government knew almost everything that everyone was doing."*

Fear of Government

- *One in two Americans (48%) say they are worried about how the Federal government will use the personal information it gathers on individuals.*
- *By a 51-38% majority, the public believes that in 10 years, "we will have lost much of our ability to keep important aspects of our lives private from government."*

Fear of Business

- *Half of all Americans (50%) are worried about whether the business community is using the personal information it gathers on individuals in a proper manner.*
- *By 72-19%, the public agrees that "most organizations that collect information about people ask for more sensitive information than is necessary."*
- *Americans' concern about their erosion of personal privacy has jumped from 48% in 1974 to 76% in December 1978 with regard to "the day they open their first charge account, take out a loan, buy something on the installment plan, or apply for a credit card."*

Sources of Improper Invasions of Privacy/Wiretapping

- *Of those members of the public who feel their privacy has been improperly invaded, 19% name the police, 16% their employer, 8% credit bureaus and 7% cite the telephone company, door-to-door salesmen and market research firms.*
- *One out of 10 Americans (9%) feel their phone has been wiretapped at some time.*

Applying for Employment, Credit, Insurance

- *17% of Americans with annual incomes of $25,000 or more say they have made a decision at one time or another **not** to apply for a job, credit or insurance because of their reluctance to provide organizations with certain types of information.*

Privacy

Biggest Invaders of Privacy

- *Drawing from a list of 18 private and public sector organizations, the following were cited as the five biggest invaders of privacy from the private sector—that is, organizations that are felt by the public to ask for too much personal information:*
  - *Finance companies (45%)*
  - *Credit bureaus (44%)*
  - *Insurance companies (38%)*
  - *Credit card companies (37%)*
  - *Newspapers, magazines and television (31%)*
- *From the public sector, Americans feel the biggest privacy invaders are:*
  - *Internal Revenue Service (38%)*
  - *CIA (34%)*
  - *FBI (33%)*
  - *Government welfare agencies (32%)*
  - *Census Bureau (24%)*
- *Private doctors (11%) and the telephone company (17%) received the least criticism.*
- *General business (that is, the non-privacy intensive industries) fare better: only one in four Americans (25%) feel that employers ask for too much personal information.*

Which Organizations Should Do More to Maintain Confidentiality of Personal Information

- *In the private sector, the public believes these organizations should do more:*
  - *Credit bureaus (45%)*
  - *Finance companies (43%)*
  - *Credit card companies (42%)*
  - *Insurance companies (37%)*
  - *Newspapers, magazines and television (34%)*
- *In the public sector, the public feels these organizations should do more:*
  - *Government welfare agencies (41%)*
  - *Internal Revenue Service (37%)*
  - *FBI (35%)*
  - *CIA (34%)*
  - *Local police (34%)*

The Employee/Employer Relationship

Propriety of Personal Information Collected

- **What the public feels is improper for an employer to ask a job applicant:**
  - *Kinds of friends the applicant has (87%)*
  - *Neighborhood applicant lives in (84%)*
  - *Information about applicant's spouse (77%)*
  - *Membership in political and community organizations (74%)*
  - *Whether applicant owns or rents residence (70%)*

- **What business information gathering practices should be illegal:**
  - *Listening in on conversations of employees to find out what they think of their supervisors (84-14% majority)*

6

- *Installing closed-circuit television to check on how fast workers perform (59-27% majority)*
- *Taking a lie-detector test (65-30% majority)*

Confidentiality

- *83% of the public feels it is "very important" that an employer should inform an employee before releasing any personal information from their files except for regular reporting of information required by law.*
- *92% of the public feels that all employers should have a specific policy designed to safeguard the information contained in employee personnel and medical files.*

Access

- *88% of the public feels that employees should have the right to look at and question supervisors' reports to management when they concern the employee's suitability for promotion. (An identical percentage of the public wants the right to examine their formal job performance reviews.)*
- *70% of the public feels that employers should not be allowed to determine employee rights regarding access to personnel files—and think a law should be passed to specify these rights.*
- *91% of employees favor a law which would require employers to inform them of any information they might have which shows that their health is being affected by conditions at work.*

The Privacy Intensive Industries	**Credit Institutions**

- *Although the public feels that **finance companies** (45%) and **credit bureaus** (44%) ask for too much personal information, they feel, on the other hand, that **credit card companies** (46%) and **banks** (63%) limit their demands for personal information.*
- *24% of the American public feels that they have been asked at one time or another by credit institutions to supply personal information that they feel was improper or unnecessary when applying for credit.*
- *What information is improper to ask when applying for credit? The American public says:*
  - *Income, salary and earnings (18%)*
  - *Credit reference (15%)*
  - *Unfair questions about job, employment (11%)*
  - *Value of assets, property (10%)*
  - *Finance; money in bank accounts (7%)*
- *One in four Americans (26%) report having been refused credit.*
- *63% say they were denied credit based on information which was unfair, 51% say the information was incomplete and 38% say the information was inaccurate.*
- *44% of Americans are not aware of their right, under the Fair Credit Reporting Act, to see their credit file when they have been refused credit.*

Insurance

- *Only finance companies and credit bureaus are perceived by the American public to be more intrusive than insurance companies.*
- *61% of the people who regulate the insurance industry—state insurance*

Privacy

commissioners—*believe that insurance companies ask individuals for too much personal information.*

- *Large majorities of the American people feel insurance companies should not ask for information about the applicant's lifestyle, moral character, income, criminal record or such obviously relevant information as whether the applicant already has life or health insurance and details of prior insurance claims.*

- *Strong majorities of the American people oppose the investigation of an applicant for health insurance to see if he or she is frequenting dangerous bars or sections of town (85%); the checking of the contents of an applicant's home to see what would be covered by a homeowners policy (73%); and the use of a central computer to find out if an applicant was ever turned down for life or health insurance (68%).*

- *65% of the public feels that the types of information insurance companies gather about applicants should be determined by law; 55% of state insurance commissioners feel similarly.*

Doctors and Hospitals

- *Only 11% of the public feels that doctors ask for too much personal information.*

- *24% of the public feels that hospitals ask for too much personal information.*

- *30% of the doctors surveyed feel they should be doing more to keep medical records confidential.*

- *39% of the doctors surveyed feel hospitals should be doing more to keep patient records confidential.*

- *91% of the public feels it should have the legal right to see their medical record, whether held by their personal doctor or by a hospital.*

The News Media

- *Only 31% of the public feels the news media ask for too much personal information.*

- *Bank executives and law enforcement officials are the most critical (78%) among all the leadership groups surveyed, feeling that the news media ask for too much personal information. Federal regulators (58%) are the least critical.*

- *70% of the public believes that the government should have the right to prosecute anyone who publishes secret materials.*

- *By a 62-25% majority, the public supports the view that the privacy of a journalist's notes and sources should be protected from the courts.*

Computers

- *54% of Americans consider the present uses of computers as an actual threat to personal privacy in this country.*

- *53% of those in the computer industry also believe that computers are a threat to personal privacy.*

- *By a 52-27% majority, the public disagrees that the privacy of personal information in computers is adequately safeguarded.*

- *63% of the public agrees with the statement that "if privacy is to be preserved, the use of computers must be sharply restricted in the future."*

- *By a 68-24% majority, the public does not feel it is justifiable to use computers to maintain a central file containing the names of all individuals who have been treated for mental health problems for use by employers.*

- *51% also feel it is not justifiable for state agencies to use computers to maintain a central file containing a record of names of individuals who have been given a prescription for a dangerous or addictive drug.*
- *A majority of all the leadership groups surveyed—except those executives in the insurance industry—believe that it is **not** justifiable for the insurance industry to use computers to keep central files containing the details of anyone who is **suspected** of making a fraudulent claim on any insurance policy.*

Government and Privacy

- *Overwhelming majorities of both the public and the leadership groups surveyed feel that a law enforcement agency **should not be able** to open the mail, tap the telephones, or look at the bank records of individuals without a court order.*
- *Majorities of the public (72%), those in Congress (84%), and federal regulatory officials (81%) feel that the police should not have the right to stop anyone on the street and demand to see some identification if the person is not doing anything illegal.*
- *Majorities of the public (58%) and law enforcement officers (67%) believe it is all right to use a lie detector to determine who has leaked confidential information from a government agency.*
- *Forty-five percent of the public are either "not too confident" or "not at all confident" that the Census Bureau protects the privacy of personal information that it collects about individuals and does not share it with other government agencies.*
- *Overwhelming majorities of the public and leadership groups think that people should have access to any files that the federal government has on them regardless of the expense and the time consumed by government agencies in responding to such requests.*
- *Fully 71% of the American people feel that it is "very important" that their states should have laws to ensure that the information in state files is kept confidential.*

Future Privacy Policy and the Business Community

- *67% of the public feels that new laws and organizational policies "could go a long way to help preserve our privacy."*
- *Because of a lack of confidence in the capacity of the courts, government, or the private sector to protect their personal privacy, fully 49% of the public feels that the main responsibility for protecting the privacy of the individual should rest with the people themselves.*
- *Business employers and executives in the credit and insurance industries don't believe comprehensive, detailed legislation is needed. These groups are divided between giving the private sector a reasonable amount of time to adopt new privacy protection measures voluntarily before legislation is enacted, and having the basic rights defined by law with specific ways of complying left up to individual companies.*
- *Government officials surveyed are more reluctant to allow the private sector time to adopt new privacy protection measures voluntarily. They prefer either having the basic rights defined by law with specific ways of complying left up to individual companies or having comprehensive and detailed legislation enacted now.*
- *Pluralities of executives in the credit and insurance industries say they want to adopt new privacy policies when a consensus is developed among employers of their type about what is right to do.*

9

Privacy

- *There are substantial minorities within the business community who want to "be a pioneer in adopting company policies." However, better than one-third (36%) of business employers say they want to wait (before adopting new privacy policies) until laws are passed "that define what is proper and improper to do, and we would then comply as good citizens."*

- *The business community is best characterized as deeply divided over what the next step to take is in privacy policy.*

- *At least 60% of the public believes that it is important to have laws regulating the type of information that organizations in the areas of credit cards (61%), medicine and health (65%), insurance (65%), employment (62%), and mailing lists (61%) can collect.*

- *Large majorities of the public (84%) and of all of the leadership groups surveyed feel that it is "very important" that organizations ask only for the information essential to making a decision.*

- *88% of the public feels that when an organization collects information on individuals, it should tell them just how that information will be used.*

- *74% of the public believes that it is important that organizations **should provide a separate written explanation** of why each piece of information is needed for anyone who asks for it.*

Chapter 1

Privacy
And The Individual

Privacy

Objectives	*Privacy is a subject of broad dimensions touching virtually every aspect of our lives. This survey focuses on individual privacy relative to government, business in general and the privacy intensive industries in particular. To put a discussion of these aspects of privacy into perspective, we must first get a sense of how the American people feel about their own personal privacy.*
1. Findings	***Level of Overall Concern With Threats to Personal Privacy*** *Concern of the American people about threats to their own personal privacy has risen dramatically in an eleven-month period.* *In January of 1978 a Harris poll showed that 47% of the public are "somewhat" concerned with threats to their personal privacy. By the time this study was conducted, approximately one year later in December 1978, this level of concern had increased 17 percentage points to 64%.* *The degree of concern about privacy varys sharply among the leadership groups studied. Government officials and doctors, both of whom have been the subject of intensive press scrutiny, are the most concerned.*
Observation	*This finding in and of itself demonstrates that privacy is an issue of serious and growing national concern. In this light the recommendations of the Federal Privacy Commission recently released are timely.*

Table 1-1	**Comparison of Concern With Threat To Privacy 1977–1978: Public & Leaders**
Question	*How concerned are you about threats to your personal privacy in America today? Would you say you're very concerned, somewhat concerned, only a little concerned or not concerned at all?*

	January 1978 *Public*	*December 1978* *Public*	*Business* *Employers*
	(1511)	*(1511)*	*(200)*
Very concerned	*25%*	*31%*	*19%*
Somewhat concerned	*22%*	*33%*	*45%*
Total Concerned	**47%**	**64%**	**64%**
Only a little concerned	*24%*	*17%*	*27%*
Not concerned at all	*28%*	*19%*	*11%*
Not sure	*1%*	*1%*	*–*

Table 1-2

Concern With Threats To Privacy: Public & Leaders

Question

How concerned are you about threats to your personal privacy in America today? Would you say you're very concerned, somewhat concerned, only a little concerned, or not concerned at all?

	(Number Respondents)	*Very Concerned*	*Somewhat Concerned*	*Only A Little Concerned*	*Not Concerned At All*
Total Public	**(1,511)**	**31%**	**33%**	**17%**	**19%**
Leaders					
Business employers	*(200)*	*19%*	*45%*	*27%*	*11%*
Privacy Intensive Industry					
Credit	*(32)*	*13%*	*44%*	*22%*	*22%*
Credit card	*(40)*	*15%*	*18%*	*30%*	*38%*
Banks	*(36)*	*8%*	*22%*	*53%*	*17%*
Insurance	*(36)*	*6%*	*36%*	*33%*	*25%*
Computer	*(36)*	*25%*	*25%*	*31%*	*19%*
Government Officials					
State insurance commissioners	*(33)*	*24%*	*27%*	*27%*	*21%*
Congress	*(77)*	*21%*	*53%*	*18%*	*8%*
Law enforcement officials	*(42)*	*24%*	*26%*	*19%*	*31%*
Regulatory officials	*(53)*	*26%*	*51%*	*17%*	*6%*
Doctors	*(33)*	*39%*	*36%*	*21%*	*3%*

2. Findings

Concern of Various Segments of the Public and Leadership Groups About Threats to Their Personal Privacy

Blacks are somewhat more concerned than whites about threats to their privacy—70% versus 63%—and the middle-of-the-road people politically are less concerned than are either liberals or conservatives. Further, those in the upper and lower income groups are less concerned than those in the middle income groups and likewise those in the middle age group (30 to 49 years) are more concerned than are those in the younger and older groups.

Within the leadership group, there is wide variance about concern with threats to personal privacy. Doctors, Congressmen or their aides, and federal regulatory officials are more concerned about threats to their personal privacy than is the public; more than 70% of these groups are "very" or "somewhat concerned." Business employers are about as concerned as the public with 64% saying they are "very" or "somewhat concerned" about threats to their personal privacy. The remaining leadership groups are less concerned about threats to their personal privacy. The least concerned leadership groups are the senior executives in credit card companies (33% "very" or "somewhat concerned") and banks (30% "very" or "somewhat concerned").

Privacy

Table 1·3	**Concern With Threats to Privacy: Public**					
Question	How concerned are you about threats to your personal privacy in America today? Would you say you're very concerned, somewhat concerned, only a little concerned, or not concerned at all?					
	(Number of Respondents)	Very Concerned	Somewhat Concerned	Only A Little Concerned	Not Concerned At All	Not Sure
Total Public	**(1,511)**	**31%**	**33%**	**17%**	**19%**	**1%**
Age						
18–29 years	(423)	29%	33%	21%	17%	1%
30–49 years	(563)	33%	36%	16%	16%	1%
50 and over	(520)	32%	29%	15%	23%	1%
Education						
8th grade or less	(136)	37%	21%	14%	26%	1%
High school	(751)	33%	32%	15%	19%	1%
College	(615)	27%	36%	21%	16%	*
Occupation						
Professional	(263)	26%	38%	21%	14%	1%
Executive	(136)	23%	35%	22%	20%	–
Proprietor	(80)	32%	34%	13%	22%	–
Skilled labor	(336)	34%	34%	12%	19%	1%
White collar	(297)	32%	29%	20%	18%	1%
Union member	(410)	34%	34%	15%	16%	1%
Race						
White	(1,316)	29%	34%	17%	19%	1%
Black	(112)	49%	21%	20%	10%	–
Income						
Under $7,000	(281)	35%	27%	15%	22%	1%
$7,000–$14,999	(421)	35%	30%	15%	18%	1%
$15,000–$24,999	(490)	29%	36%	19%	16%	1%
$25,000 and over	(231)	23%	36%	21%	20%	–
Political Philosophy						
Conservative	(488)	36%	30%	14%	20%	*
Middle-of-the-road	(568)	25%	36%	20%	18%	1%
Liberal	(263)	34%	35%	18%	12%	–

*Less than 0.5%

| 3. Findings | **Should Privacy be a Basic "Right" in this Society** |

As another dimension to the measure of the concern of Americans for their privacy, the public was asked whether or not the right to privacy should be added to the list of rights to life, liberty and the pursuit of happiness.

By a sizable 76% to 17% majority the American people say that the right to privacy should be added to this list. But leadership groups do not feel nearly as strongly as the public in this regard.

| **Observation** | *In the area of privacy – as in other important areas–the public seems to be leading the leaders.* |

| **Table 1-4** | **Privacy as a Fundamental Right: Public and Leaders** |

| **Question** | *The United States was founded on the belief that the rights to life, liberty, and the pursuit of happiness were fundamental for both the individual and a just society. Do you think we should or should not add today the right to privacy to this list?* |

	(Number of Respondents)	Should Add	Should Not	Not Sure
Total Public	**(1,511)**	**76%**	**17%**	**7%**
Leaders				
Business employers	(200)	55%	38%	8%
Privacy Intensive Industry				
Credit	(32)	50%	41%	9%
Credit card	(40)	45%	55%	–
Banks	(36)	31%	67%	3%
Insurance	(35)	43%	54%	3%
Computer	(36)	67%	28%	6%
Government Officials				
State insurance commissioners	(32)	47%	44%	9%
Congress	(77)	48%	48%	4%
Law enforcement officials	(42)	33%	60%	7%
Regulatory officials	(53)	60%	34%	6%
Doctors	(33)	58%	36%	6%

| 4. Findings | **Personal Relationships in a Privacy Context** |

Most Americans feel they have maintained a balance between their need for privacy and their need for a social contact.

A substantial majority (88%) feel they are generally able to be by themselves when they need to be. A smaller majority of the public (67%) also do not feel that there is so much noise in today's world that they have little peace and quiet. Most (89%) of the public do not feel that their neighbors know too much about their personal lives. Fully 94% feel they have someone they can share their personal problems with when they need to, and 84% feel they have contact with people who care about them.

By a 79–10% majority the public does not feel that their employers know too many personal things about them. By an 84–14% majority they do not feel that someone is watching or recording what they do. Finally, by a 70–24% majority, they do not feel that some decisions are being made wrongly about them on the basis of information that they don't know about.

Privacy

Observation:	Clearly the American people as a whole do not feel paranoid about their personal privacy. They feel they have privacy when they want it and social contact when they want it. In this	context, then, their concern about institution-based threats to personal privacy cannot be discounted.

Table 1-5 — **Whether Various Statements Express the Way You Feel: Public**

Question — Now, I'd like to read you some more statements. Please say for each one if it expresses the way you yourself feel, or not.

(Number of respondents: 1,511)	Expresses The Way I Feel	Does Not	Not Sure
I have someone I can share my personal problems with when I need to	94%	6%	1%
I am generally able to be by myself when I need to be	88%	11%	1%
There is so much noise in today's world that I have little peace and quiet	31%	67%	2%
I think some decisions are being made wrongly about me on the basis of information that I don't know about	24%	70%	6%
I don't have much contact with people who care about me	15%	84%	2%
I sometimes feel someone is watching me or recording what I do	14%	84%	2%
My employer knows too many personal things about me	10%	79%	10%
My neighbors know too much about my personal life	9%	89%	2%

5. Findings

Privacy and Morality

For the most part, majorities of Americans believe that "non-public" activities of a "moral" nature should be left to the individual to decide, and should not be decided by law.

For example, large majorities of the public believe that homosexual relations in private between consenting adults (70%) and heterosexual relations between unmarried adults (79%) are areas of private choice that should be left to the individual and not regulated or forbidden by law. Smaller but still sizable majorities feel similarly about an individual's decision to have an abortion (59%) and to smoke marijuana (55%). With the exception of law enforcement officials, on abortions and marijuana, the leaders are in accord with the public that these activities should be left to the individual.

The public is less willing to agree that those types of activities that have a public dimension should be left to private choice and consent. Only 35% feel that engaging in prostitution should be left to the individual, and only 24% feel that the selling of pornographic magazines and films should be left to the individual. Again, with the exception of law enforcement officials, leaders are less likely than the public to believe that prostitution and the sale of pornography should be totally forbidden by law and more likely to feel these activities should be regulated by law.

Among neither the public nor the leaders do majorities feel that either of these activities should be totally left to the individual.

Table 1-6

Whether Specific Activities Should be Matter of Private Choice: Public and Leaders

Question

I will read you some activities that some people feel are matters of private choice or consent that ought to be left to the individual, other people feel should be regulated by law, and others feel should be forbidden by law altogether. As I read each activity, please tell me which of the phrases on this card describes how **you** *feel that activity should be treated—should it be left to the individual, should it be allowed, but regulated by law, or should it be totally forbidden by law?*

| | | Leaders | | | | | | | | | | |
| | | Privacy Intensive Industries | | | | | Government Officials | | | | |
(Number of respondents)	Total Public (1,512)	Business Employers (199)	Credit (32)	Credit Card (40)	Banks (36)	Insurance (36)	Computer (36)	State Insurance Commissioners (33)	Congress (77)	Law Enforcement Officials (42)	Regulatory Officials (53)	Doctors (33)
	%	%	%	%	%	%	%	%	%	%	%	%
Heterosexual relations between unmarried adults												
Left to the individual	79	94	100	98	100	97	92	88	96	88	98	100
Allowed but regulated by law	3	3	–	–	–	–	–	3	1	5	–	–
Totally forbidden by law	13	1	–	–	–	3	8	6	3	5	2	–
Not sure	5	2	–	3	–	–	–	3	–	2	–	–
Homosexual relations in private between consenting adults												
Left to the individual	70	90	91	88	89	92	83	82	91	69	96	97
Allowed but regulated by law	5	5	–	3	6	–	3	3	5	7	–	3
Totally forbidden by law	20	4	6	8	6	8	11	15	4	21	4	–
Not sure	5	2	3	3	–	–	3	–	–	2	–	–
Having an abortion												
Left to the individual	59	72	84	83	75	83	67	70	60	45	74	76
Allowed but regulated by law	17	22	13	10	22	11	25	18	29	33	25	18
Totally forbidden by law	21	5	3	3	–	6	6	12	10	21	2	6
Not sure	3	2	–	5	3	–	3	–	1	–	–	–
Smoking marijuana in a private residence												
Left to the individual	55	73	63	70	58	61	72	58	65	36	70	67
Allowed but regulated by law	14	13	13	10	19	17	14	6	22	21	17	27
Totally forbidden by law	29	13	25	18	19	19	14	36	12	43	8	6
Not sure	2	2	–	3	3	3	–	–	1	–	6	–
Engaging in prostitution												
Left to the individual	35	40	38	43	33	44	22	30	17	5	32	45
Allowed but regulated by law	24	43	31	35	42	33	47	21	57	33	53	45
Totally forbidden by law	37	16	25	20	19	22	28	42	23	62	11	6
Not sure	4	2	6	3	6	–	3	6	3	–	4	3
Riding a motorcycle without a protective helmet												
Left to the individual	34	42	47	53	58	33	53	52	34	26	33	36
Allowed but regulated by law	23	22	25	18	8	25	17	6	25	31	15	21
Totally forbidden by law	41	34	25	23	33	36	31	39	42	40	52	42
Not sure	1	3	3	8	–	6	–	3	–	2	–	–
Selling pornographic magazines and films in bookstores												
Left to the individual	24	25	31	38	22	28	23	24	12	2	28	30
Allowed but regulated by law	30	47	44	30	44	50	54	39	79	36	57	64
Totally forbidden by law	44	27	22	30	31	22	23	33	7	60	15	6
Not sure	2	1	3	3	3	–	–	3	3	2	–	–

Privacy

| **6. Findings** | **Personal Privacy in Various Living Environments** |

Among the American public, the largest percentages feel that the most privacy is to be found either in the anonymity of large cities (29%) or in the sparsely settled rural areas of the country (37%). Most Americans do not believe that the small towns or the suburbs are conducive to personal privacy.

| **Table 1-7** | **Where People Have the Most Personal Privacy: Public** |

| **Question** | Do you think that people have the most personal privacy in rural areas, small towns, large cities, or the suburbs of large cities? |

			Region		
(Number of respondents)	Total Public (1,500)	East (430)	Mid-west (403)	South (404)	West (263)
Rural areas	37%	34%	42%	41%	29%
Small towns	13%	9%	9%	16%	20%
Large cities	29%	32%	30%	26%	31%
Suburbs of large cities	11%	15%	10%	10%	8%
Not sure	10%	10%	9%	7%	12%

| **7. Findings** | **Actual Experiences With Invasions of Privacy** |

Almost four in five Americans say they have **never** been victims of what they felt were improper invasions of privacy. However, the 19% represents no less than 29 million Americans who feel their privacy has been invaded.

| **Observation** | Despite this lack of experience, government and business should not be content to rest on their laurels. As seen earlier, two in three Americans are concerned about the potential for their privacy being invaded. And this should be viewed as a very real concern. |

Government officials, perhaps because they are in the public eye, are much more likely to think their privacy has been invaded than the public—23% versus 14% for the public. Over 35% of those in government—and particularly law enforcement officials (55%)—say their privacy has been invaded improperly.

| **Observation** | A clear implication of these findings is that those leaders who are most frequently the subject of the attention of the media are the most likely to feel their privacy has been invaded. |

Table 1-8	**Whether Privacy Has Been Invaded: Public and Leaders**			
Question	Have you personally ever been the victim of what you felt was an improper invasion of privacy?			

	(Number Of Respondents)	Yes, Have Been	No, Never Have Been	Not Sure
Total Public	**(1,513)**	**19%**	**78%**	**3%**
Leaders				
Business employers	(200)	23%	74%	4%
Privacy Intensive Industry				
Credit	(32)	22%	72%	6%
Credit card	(40)	15%	83%	3%
Banks	(36)	19%	81%	–
Insurance	(36)	17%	83%	–
Computer	(36)	25%	75%	–
Government Officials				
State insurance commissioners	(33)	36%	61%	3%
Congress	(76)	39%	54%	7%
Law enforcement officials	(42)	55%	43%	2%
Regulatory officials	(53)	36%	62%	2%
Doctors	(33)	39%	58%	3%

Those among the public who feel their privacy has been invaded improperly most often cite police departments (19%), and their employer (16%) as invaders of their privacy.

Table 1-9	**Organizations Involved in Invasions of Privacy: Public and Leaders**
	(Base: Feel privacy has been invaded)
Question	What type of organization or authority was involved in this invasion of privacy? Any other?

	Total Public
(Number of respondents)	(272)
Police department; police searching without warrants	19%
Company, place of employment, employer	16%
Credit bureau	8%
Telephone/door-to-door sales pitches, market research	7%
Government	6%
Insurance company	6%
Personal gossip, relatives	6%
Invasion of home by various people, neighbors	5%
Internal Revenue Service	4%
Hospital	3%
School	3%
Church	3%
Junk mail, mail order	2%
State government	2%
Burglary	2%
Collection agencies	1%
The press/media	–
Any other answer	20%
Not sure	2%

Privacy

8. Findings	**Wiretapping**

Almost one in 10 Americans (9%) feel their phone has been wiretapped at some time. This figure is down slightly from 12% in January 1978.

Government officials are much more likely than the public, executives in the privacy intensive industries, or business employers, to believe that their telephones have been tapped.

Table 1-10	**Whether Telephone Has Been Tapped: Public and Leaders**

Question	Do you believe that your telephone has ever been tapped or not?

	(Number Of Respondents)	Yes, Has Been Tapped	No, Has Not Been Tapped	Not, Sure/ Don't Know
Total Public				
December 1978	**(1,505)**	**9%**	**85%**	**7%**
January 1978	**(1,458)**	**12%**	**86%**	**2%**
Leaders				
Business employers	(199)	9%	81%	10%
Privacy Intensive Industry				
Credit	(32)	6%	81%	13%
Credit card	(40)	8%	85%	8%
Banks	(36)	8%	86%	6%
Insurance	(36)	6%	92%	3%
Computer	(36)	8%	75%	17%
Government Officials				
State insurance commissioners	(33)	33%	42%	24%
Congress	(77)	39%	45%	16%
Law enforcement officials	(42)	24%	62%	14%
Regulatory officials	(53)	25%	64%	11%
Doctors	(32)	13%	81%	6%

Table 1-11	**Whether Personal Privacy is Surrendered When Applying for Credit: Public Trend**

Question	I would like you to tell me whether you agree or disagree with the following statement: Americans begin surrendering their personal privacy the day they open their first charge account, take out a loan, buy something on the installment plan, or apply for a credit card.

Total Public	December 1978	January 1978	1977	1976	1974
Agree	76%	71%	67%	47%	48%
Disagree	21%	24%	24%	47%	43%
Not Sure	3%	5%	9%	6%	9%

Chapter 2

Personal Privacy
In Relation To
Governmental And
Business Institutions

Privacy

Objectives	*The first chapter of this study was concerned with how the public and those in leadership positions in industry and government feel about various aspects of their own personal privacy.*
	This chapter focuses on how they feel business and governmental groups impact on personal privacy, which organizations are handling the individuals personal data responsibly, and which are not.

---

1. Findings

Degree to Which the Public Trusts Government and Business in the Handling of Personal Information

The public is worried about how business and government handles the personal information it collects about individuals.

Table 2-1

Whether Trust Government to Use Personal Information Properly: Public

Question

On the whole, when it comes to the federal government collecting personal information about you, would you say you pretty much trust them to use it properly, or that you are worried about how they will use it?

	Business	Government
Total public	*(1511)*	*(1511)*
Pretty much trust them	36%	38%
Worried	50%	48%
It depends	9%	10%
Not sure	4%	4%

---

2. Findings

Perceptions of Same General Issues Regarding the Collection and Use of Personal Data by Public and Private Institutions

Americans are convinced that most organizations collect more sensitive information than is necessary—by 72% to 19%—and that some people are prevented from getting fair treatment because of past mistakes being kept too long on their records—by 81% to 11%.

By the same token, the public is not convinced (by a slim 50% to 46% plurality,) that a great deal of sensitive information has to be collected in order to provide credit, insurance or employment. The public is divided on whether or not there are enough checks and safeguards against the misuse of personal data.

Observation

Earlier we saw that the public is generally concerned about threats to their personal privacy. Now it becomes apparent that one of the things the public is quite concerned about

specifically is how public and private institutions handle the personal data they collect about individuals.

The public also believes that effective law enforcement requires some intrusion into personal lives—57% to 36%—and that consumers begin surrendering their privacy the moment they apply for credit.

The leadership groups, in varying degrees, are in general agreement with the public that effective law enforcement requires some intrusions into personal lives, that some people are prevented from getting fair treatment because of past mistakes remaining on their records too long, and that people who complain about their privacy are not engaged in immoral or illegal conduct. Majorities of all leadership groups, except banking and credit card company executives, join the public in agreeing that Americans begin surrendering their personal privacy on the day they open their first charge account, take out a loan, buy something on the installment plan, or apply for a credit card.

However, the leadership groups are divided in their agreement on some key statements. For example, while majorities of executives in credit card companies, banks, insurance companies, and the computer industry separate themselves from the public by agreeing that it is proper to collect a great deal of sensitive information in order to provide credit, insurance, and employment, majorities of the Congressional and federal regulatory samples side with the public by disagreeing with the statement. Business employers also disagree by almost the same margin as the public, and doctors disagree by a somewhat wider margin.

The leaders in the privacy intensive industries are clearly at odds with other leadership groups and the public on two items. First, they disagree that most organizations collecting information about people ask for more sensitive information than necessary. Second, majorities of leaders in the privacy intensive industries are also at odds with the public, business employers, and government officials in believing that most organizations that use information about people have enough checks and safeguards against the misuse of personal information.

Privacy

| Table 2-2 | **Agreement With Various Privacy-Related Statements: Public and Leaders** |
| Question | *I am going to read you some statements. I would like you to tell me whether you agree or disagree with each one.* |

| | | | Leaders | | | | | | | | | |
| | | | Privacy Intensive Industries | | | | | Government Officials | | | | |
(Number of respondents)	Total Public (1,512)	Business Employers (199)	Credit (32)	Credit Card (40)	Banks (36)	Insurance (36)	Computer (36)	State Insurance Commissioners (33)	Congress (77)	Law Enforcement Officials (42)	Regulatory Officials (53)	Doctors (32)
	%	%	%	%	%	%	%	%	%	%	%	%
Some people are prevented from getting fair treatment because of past mistakes kept too long on their record												
Agree	81	75	53	55	56	75	75	73	87	68	81	78
Disagree	11	16	38	35	39	19	8	18	9	29	9	13
Not sure	8	10	9	10	6	6	17	9	4	2	9	9
Americans begin surrendering their personal privacy the day they open their first charge account, take out a loan, buy something on the installment plan, or apply for a credit card												
Agree	76	78	66	50	44	69	92	76	88	74	81	75
Disagree	21	22	31	50	53	31	8	21	10	21	17	22
Not sure	3	–	3	–	3	–	–	3	1	5	2	3
Most organizations that collect information about people ask for more sensitive information than is necessary												
Agree	72	65	31	25	14	33	44	73	•73	52	75	75
Disagree	19	29	69	73	83	61	47	24	13	38	19	19
Not sure	9	6	–	3	3	6	8	3	14	10	6	6
In order to have effective law enforcement, everyone should be prepared to accept some intrusions into their personal lives												
Agree	57	81	84	83	74	81	67	79	62	83	67	88
Disagree	36	17	13	15	20	14	28	12	31	17	29	9
Not sure	7	2	3	3	6	6	6	9	6	–	4	3
In order to provide credit, insurance, or employment, it is proper to collect a great deal of sensitive, personal information about people												
Agree	46	46	50	68	64	69	69	52	34	55	33	44
Disagree	50	51	50	25	36	25	28	45	60	38	60	56
Not sure	4	3	–	8	–	6	3	3	6	7	8	–
Most organizations that use information about people have enough checks and safeguards against the misuse of personal information												
Agree	41	33	50	70	67	58	28	27	26	24	8	6
Disagree	41	56	34	23	28	25	53	61	62	59	85	63
Not sure	18	12	16	8	6	17	19	12	12	17	8	31
Most people who complain about their privacy are engaged in immoral or illegal conduct												
Agree	27	6	9	5	6	6	3	3	1	15	2	9
Disagree	64	86	81	95	86	89	94	94	97	76	94	91
Not sure	10	8	9	–	8	6	3	3	1	10	4	–

3. Findings

Willingness to Provide Personal Information in Return for Employment, Credit or Insurance

Fourteen percent of the American people, at some time in their lives, decided not to apply for a job, credit or insurance because they did not want to provide certain personal information.

Observation

We recognize that much of privacy is concerned with "trade-offs"—what people are willing to give by way of personal information in order to enjoy a particular quality of life.

While 14% may not be a dramatic number, certainly it must be viewed as an early warning signal to government and industry that other ways must be found to qualify people for jobs or evaluate them for credit or insurance.

*Those who decide **not** to give up certain personal information in order to apply for a job, credit or insurance are more likely to be those who are politically liberal, younger and college educated. More people living in the western United States hold this attitude.*

Table 2-3

Whether Have Ever Not Applied for Something Due to Required Personal Information: Public

Question

*Have you ever decided **not** to apply for something, like a job, credit, or insurance, because you did not want to provide certain kinds of information about yourself?*

	(Number Of Respondents)	Yes, Did Not Apply	No	Can't Remember/ Not Sure
Total Public	**(1,496)**	**14%**	**85%**	**1%**
Region				
East	(426)	14%	85%	1%
Midwest	(404)	15%	85%	1%
South	(399)	9%	90%	1%
West	(267)	22%	76%	2%
Age				
18–29 years	(423)	19%	79%	2%
30–49 years	(557)	16%	82%	2%
50 and over	(510)	8%	92%	1%
Education				
8th grade or less	(136)	3%	96%	1%
High school	(743)	14%	85%	1%
College	(607)	17%	82%	1%
Income				
Under $7,000	(281)	11%	88%	1%
$7,000–$14,999	(418)	14%	85%	1%
$15,000–$24,999	(485)	15%	83%	1%
$25,000 and over	(227)	17%	83%	1%
Political Philosophy				
Conservative	(483)	12%	87%	1%
Middle-of-the-road	(564)	12%	87%	1%
Liberal	(257)	22%	78%	*
Religion				
Protestant	(709)	10%	89%	1%
Catholic	(403)	13%	86%	1%
Jewish	(63)	25%	72%	3%

*Less than 0.5%

Privacy

As might be expected, most of those who did not want to give up their personal information (91%) did so because they felt that the request for this information was unfair.

Table 2-4

Whether Fair to Require Personal Information on Application: Public
(Base: Have not applied for something because personal information required)

Question

Did you feel that it was fair or unfair for that information to be required on the application?

	Total Public
(Number of respondents)	*(210)*
Fair	*7%*
Unfair	*91%*
Not sure	*2%*

4. Findings

Which Governmental and Private Sector Organizations are Thought to Ask for Too Much Personal Information

Finance companies and **credit bureaus** *(45% and 44% respectively)* are the organizations most often cited as asking for too much personal information. Thirty-seven percent of the public feel that **credit card companies** ask for too much personal information ranking these organizations fifth overall in this regard. **Banking institutions** are the most well thought-of in the credit and finance institutions, but three in 10 Americans *(29%)* still feel the banks ask for too much personal information.

The **insurance industry** also receives a good deal of criticism. While a majority *(54%)* feel that insurance companies limit their demands, 38% of Americans feel that they ask for too much personal information. This rating places the insurance industry in a tie with the **IRS** as the third most criticized type of organization.

Employers receive much less criticism, with 25% of the public feeling that employers ask for too much information.

Governmental institutions receive varying degrees of criticism. For some organizations such as the CIA, the FBI, and Congressional committees, there are large percentages of respondents who are not sure whether these organizations ask for too much personal information or not. It is important to note that while the percentages who feel that the CIA and FBI ask for too much information are not as high as those who feel this way about elements about the private sector. They are pluralities. Regardless, the Internal Revenue Service is the most criticized of the governmental organizations; 38% of the public feel it asks for too much personal information. The next most criticized governmental institutions are the CIA *(34%)*, the FBI *(33%)*, and government welfare agencies *(32%)*. The Census Bureau *(24%)*, local police *(23%)*, Congressional committees *(22%)*, and the Social Security Administration *(21%)* are criticized by less than a quarter of the public.

Private doctors *(11%)* and the **telephone company** *(17%)* receive the least criticism.

Virtually all of the leadership groups are much more critical than the public of the news media and Congressional committees. Exceptions are those in Congress who (with only 22% feeling that Congressional committees ask for too much personal information) are in agreement with the public and are the least critical of all leadership groups on this measure.

However, executives in the credit and insurance industries are much less critical of all other organizations—especially credit organizations—than are the general public, those in Congress, state insurance commissioners, and federal regulatory officials.

Despite all of the recent legislation in the credit area that relates to the protection of individual privacy, 61% of Congressmen and their aides are critical of credit bureaus and 60% are critical of finance companies for asking for too much personal information. These percentages are much higher than those for the general public. Congressmen and their aides are less critical of banks (35%) and credit card companies (40%) than they are of credit bureaus and finance companies. Nevertheless, they are still more likely than the public to feel these organizations ask for too much personal information.

While only 17% of executives in the insurance industry feel that insurance companies ask for too much information, 61% of state insurance commissioners, 47% of Congressmen and their aides, and 49% of federal regulatory officials feel that too much information is requested.

Law enforcement officials are less likely than the general public to feel that either the FBI or the CIA ask for too much information. However, at 21% they are only marginally less likely than the general public (23%) to feel that the local police ask for too much personal information. A very high 78% feel the news media ask for too much information.

Employers (17%) are less likely than the general public (25%), those in Congress (23%), and federal regulatory officials (45%), to feel that employers are asking for too much personal information.

Private doctors generally agree with the public about the degree to which private doctors and hospitals ask for too much personal information.

Observation

Despite the enormous amount of news coverage in the past decade on violations of individual privacy by law enforcement agencies such as the FBI, the public is more concerned about threats to personal privacy by the credit and insurance industries and the IRS than it is about law enforcement institutions, especially the local police.

With the exception of the news media and Congressional committees, the public is generally more critical of organizations on each measure than are executives in these organizations. Government officials (excluding law enforcement officials) in turn, are generally more critical of organizations than the public.

The Congress and federal regulatory officials are especially critical of the credit industry despite the fact that there has already been some regulation in this area. State insurance commissioners are highly critical of the insurance industry.

Privacy

| | Table 2-5 | | **Which Organizations Ask For Too Much Personal Information: Public and Leaders** |

Question

I am going to read you a list of organizations and individuals which sometimes collect or use information about us. For each of these I would like you to tell me whether you feel they limit their personal information about individuals to what is really necessary or whether they ask for too much personal information

| | | Leaders | | | | | | | | | | |
| | | Privacy Intensive Industries | | | | | Government Officials | | | | |
(Number of respondents)	Total Public (1,512)	Business Employers (200)	Credit (32)	Credit Card (40)	Banks (36)	Insur-ance (36)	Com-puter (36)	State Insurance Commis-sioners (33)	Congress (77)	Law Enforce-ment Offi-cials (42)	Regu-latory Offi-cials (53)	Doctors (33)
	%	%	%	%	%	%	%	%	%	%	%	%
Finance companies	45	46	16	20	3	22	42	47	60	31	51	39
Credit bureaus	44	45	19	13	8	33	44	64	61	43	55	52
Insurance companies	38	27	13	23	3	17	39	61	47	24	49	42
Internal Revenue Service	38	27	25	23	11	25	25	42	31	21	26	33
Credit card companies	37	33	6	8	3	19	22	27	40	19	38	39
The CIA	34	27	31	20	6	22	11	22	36	17	32	36
The FBI	33	29	19	25	11	25	28	38	53	21	47	45
Government welfare agencies	32	22	19	8	11	28	19	18	42	17	47	24
Newspapers, magazines, and television	31	69	75	65	78	72	42	68	60	78	58	61
Banks	29	27	3	10	–	17	33	36	35	19	36	33
Employers	25	17	6	13	3	19	14	27	23	21	45	30
Hospitals	24	17	16	5	3	11	17	18	19	14	32	21
The Census Bureau	24	32	13	23	28	17	25	52	39	21	17	30
Local police	23	11	9	13	6	6	11	6	35	21	36	12
Congressional committees	22	57	47	45	50	63	36	45	22	37	60	42
Social Security Administration	21	10	3	3	–	11	6	15	17	7	13	18
The telephone company	17	9	–	10	3	11	11	9	13	10	19	15
Private doctors	11	3	–	–	–	3	6	3	9	7	11	9

5. Findings

Comparison of Industry and Public Views as to Which Industries Ask for Too Much General Information

The following table shows the difference between what the public thinks of a particular industry and what the industry executives think of their own industry in terms of whether or not that industry asks for too much personal information.

The difference can be viewed as the degree to which industry executives are out of touch with the public.

Banks and credit card company executives would appear to be most out of touch with consumers with a difference of 29 percentage points. Credit bureau executives and insurance company executives, with 25 to 21 point differentials respectively, are also not very well in tune with consumers.

Employers, the Congress, police and law enforcement officials, as well as private doctors, appear to be very closely in touch with consumers as to whether or not they ask for too much personal information.

Observation

Clearly credit card companies, banks, insurance companies and credit bureaus must listen more closely to what consumers have to say if they are to win the confidence of the public.

Table 2-6	**Public and Leadership Attitudes to the Intrusiveness of Various Industries and Groups**

Percentages of Leaders in each category who believe their own industry/group "asks for too much information."

	By Executives of the Industry	By the Public	Difference
Credit Card Companies	8	37	29
Credit Bureaus	19	44	25
Insurance Companies	17	38	21
Banks	–	29	29
Employers	17	25	6
Congress	22	22	–
Police/Law Enforcement	21	23	2
Private Doctors	9	11	2

6. Findings

Whether these Organizations are Doing Enough to Maintain the Confidentiality of the Personal Information They Collect

With minor differences, the extent to which the public and leadership groups feel the industries collect too much personal information is the extent to which they feel those same industries should be doing more to protect the confidentiality of that information.

Table 2-7	**Which Organizations Should Be Doing More to Maintain Confidentiality of Personal Information: Public and Leaders**

Question

Now I'm going to read you the same list of organizations again. This time I would like you to tell me whether each organization is currently doing enough to keep the personal information they have on individuals confidential, or should they be doing more?

			Leaders									
			Privacy Intensive Industries					Government Officials				
(Number of respondents)	Total Public (1,512)	Business Employers (200)	Credit (32)	Credit Card (40)	Banks (36)	Insur-ance (36)	Com-puter (36)	State Insurance Commis-sioners (33)	Congress (77)	Law Enforce-ment Offi-cials (42)	Regu-latory Offi-cials (53)	Doctors (33)
	%	%	%	%	%	%	%	%	%	%	%	%
Credit bureaus	45	52	31	23	14	36	69	66	60	40	62	64
Finance companies	43	43	13	20	11	28	57	61	56	40	50	50
Credit card companies	42	44	22	18	11	28	54	44	53	36	58	52
Government welfare agencies	41	36	31	20	3	33	37	38	40	19	49	41
Internal Revenue Service	37	43	38	33	22	33	39	44	42	21	44	52
Insurance companies	37	30	13	13	8	11	43	59	44	26	60	52
The FBI	35	38	31	23	6	28	34	35	42	17	48	38
The CIA	34	32	19	20	11	23	31	23	32	15	35	34
Newspapers, magazines, and television	34	X	X	X	X	X	X	X	X	X	X	X
Local police	34	24	19	20	11	25	29	35	52	21	54	26
Congressional committees	31	59	50	45	61	65	51	53	53	44	65	50
Banks	30	26	6	15	11	14	41	47	44	21	54	33
Employers	29	26	16	20	8	23	40	50	39	24	52	30
Social Security Administration	27	18	6	10	6	14	20	25	25	7	27	23
The Census Bureau	26	26	19	23	17	8	20	31	22	19	17	25
Hospitals	23	19	13	10	6	11	29	31	26	15	30	39
The telephone company	22	12	3	18	3	11	22	26	23	12	24	21
Private doctors	17	13	9	3	8	17	14	19	21	10	18	30

X = Not asked of leaders

Privacy

Table 2-8	Whether Various Organizations Collect Too Much Personal Information: Public
Question	I am going to read you a list of organizations and individuals which sometimes collect or use information about us. For each of these I would like you to tell me whether you feel they limit their personal information about individuals to what is really necessary or whether they ask for too much personal information.

(Number of respondents: 1,512)	Ask For Too Much	Limit Their Demands	Not Sure
Finance companies	45%	33%	22%
Credit bureaus	44%	31%	25%
Insurance companies	38%	54%	9%
Internal Revenue Service	38%	50%	13%
Credit card companies	37%	46%	17%
The CIA	34%	20%	47%
The FBI	33%	31%	37%
Government welfare agencies	32%	43%	25%
Newspapers, magazines and television	31%	45%	24%
Banks	29%	63%	8%
Employers	25%	64%	11%
Hospitals	24%	69%	6%
The Census Bureau	24%	61%	15%
Local police	23%	62%	16%
Congressional committees	22%	33%	45%
Social Security Administration	21%	58%	21%
Telephone company	17%	70%	13%
Private doctors	11%	84%	5%

Table 2-9	Whether Various Organizations Are Doing Enough To Maintain Confidentiality of Personal Information: Public
Question	Now I'm going to read you the same list of organizations again. This time I would like you to tell me whether each organization is currently doing enough to keep the personal information they have on individuals confidential, or should they be doing more?

(Number of respondents: 1,504)	Should Be Doing More	Doing Enough	Not Sure
Credit bureaus	45%	30%	25%
Finance companies	43%	34%	23%
Credit card companies	42%	38%	21%
Government welfare agencies	41%	35%	25%
Internal Revenue Service	37%	44%	19%
Insurance companies	37%	49%	14%
The FBI	35%	31%	34%
The CIA	34%	25%	41%
Newspapers, magazines and television	34%	40%	27%
Local police	34%	48%	18%
Congressional committees	31%	27%	42%
Banks	30%	58%	12%
Employers	29%	56%	15%
Social Security Administration	27%	49%	24%
Census Bureau	26%	52%	22%
Hospitals	23%	66%	11%
Telephone company	22%	62%	17%
Private doctors	17%	75%	8%

Chapter 3

Privacy

Objectives

The next few chapters deal with privacy intensive industries.

Specifically, the objectives of this chapter are to explore three dimensions of the employer/employee relationship that relate to privacy—the propriety of the personal information that is collected by employers, the extent to which employers keep personal information confidential, and employees' rights to have access to information about themselves held by their employers.

---

1. Findings

What Personal Information It Is Proper For Employers To Collect

In the previous chapter, it was shown that one in four employees think their employers collect too much personal information.

The public and the leadership groups are adamant that employers should not ask job applicants or seek information on the kinds of friends applicants have, the type of neighborhood in which they live, or information about their spouses or their membership in political or community organizations.

It is not surprising that over half the public and leaders also believe that employers should not collect information such as race, credit-worthiness, records of arrest without conviction, the results of psychological tests and whether or not applicants own or rent their homes.

The public does recognize the employer's need for information concerning educational background, employment history, and test results which measure a person's ability to perform certain jobs.

What is surprising is that on almost every item, employers are more likely than either the full-time employed or congressional respondents to feel that it is improper for employers to ask job applicants certain types of information. In some instances, the differences separating employers from the full-time employed are quite large. For example, by 26 percentage points, business employers (50%) are more likely than the full-time employed (24%) to feel that seeking a person's age when he applies for employment is improper. On three items—drinking habits, height and weight, and evaluations of mental stability—employers are at least 18 percentage points more likely than full-time employees to feel that asking for this information is improper.

Observation

It is apparent that employers have been sensitized to the issue of what information it is proper to ask for in a job application situation.

To their credit, employers seem to recognize that they will have to seek other than the traditional ways to determine whether or not an applicant would make a good employee.

		Public		**Leaders**	

Table 3-1   **Various Types of Information Considered Improper to Ask Job Applicant: Public and Leaders**

Question   *Now I'd like to ask you some questions about* **the subject of employment**. *When someone applies for a job, do you think that it is proper for an employer to ask for the following types of information or not? Please think of most jobs in business and government, not jobs which require security clearances or special moral qualities.*

	Public		*Leaders*	
(Number of respondents)	*Total* (1,513)	*Full-Time Employed* (612)	*Business Employers* (200)	*Congress* (77)
What kinds of friends the applicant has	87%	92%	97%	91%
The type of neighborhood in which the applicant lives	84%	86%	96%	87%
Information about the applicant's spouse	77%	78%	85%	74%
Membership in political and community organizations	74%	76%	83%	70%
Whether the applicant owns or rents residence	70%	73%	81%	64%
Records of arrest without conviction	62%	69%	86%	82%
General credit-worthiness and ability to pay bills	54%	58%	65%	58%
The results of psychological tests	52%	54%	62%	71%
Race	52%	57%	74%	66%
Whether the applicant has ever received psychiatric or psychological counseling	50%	54%	62%	65%
Whether the applicant is pregnant or not	42%	48%	64%	57%
Marital status	42%	45%	57%	40%
Whether the applicant uses illegal drugs	41%	46%	48%	60%
Drinking habits	38%	43%	61%	52%
Height and weight	37%	36%	54%	45%
Evaluations of mental stability	36%	39%	57%	62%
The applicant's military discharge status	36%	38%	40%	35%
Sex	29%	32%	52%	36%
Age	22%	24%	50%	31%
Medical reports on current physical condition and past medical history	21%	21%	17%	30%
References from the applicant's former employer	12%	13%	7%	1%
The results of tests which measure the ability of people to do different types of jobs	11%	10%	18%	9%
Employment history	9%	8%	–	–
Educational background	6%	6%	–	–

33

Privacy

2. Findings

Should Certain Information Gathering Practices Be Illegal?

A large majority of both the public and employers disapprove of three of the items:

- *By an 84–14% majority, employees believe that the practice of listening in on the conversations of employees to find out what they think about their supervisors or managers should be forbidden by law. Seventy percent of employers and 77% of Congressmen or their aides concur with this feeling.*

- *By a 69–27% majority, employees feel that the practice of installing closed circuit television to obtain continuous checks on how fast workers perform should also be forbidden by law. However, many fewer business employers (45%) and even fewer of those in Congress (34%) share this opinion.*

- *By a 65–30% majority, employees also believe that asking a job applicant to take a lie detector test should be forbidden by law. A somewhat smaller majority of business employers (55%) and Congressional respondents (60%) share this judgment.*

The views of employees are less definitive on other items:

- *Employees divide 50–40% in favor of having a law which forbids employers from asking a job applicant to take a psychological test. Congressional respondents are also divided (49–45%) with a slight plurality feeling that the practice should not be forbidden by law. Employers differ from the views of both groups with 69% saying that the practice should not be forbidden by law.*

- *Employees are also divided (47–46%) on whether a law should be enacted which would forbid an employer from requiring an employee to take a lie detector test when there is suspicion of theft in his department. A slim majority of business employers (56%) and those in Congress (52%) feel there should not be such a law.*

- *There is a slight majority of employees (51%) who feel that employers should not be forbidden by law from using closed circuit television to prevent theft. A large majority of business employers (77%) and Congressional respondents (77%) concur.*

Observation

Generally, the public is wary about what might be termed "formalized eavesdropping", be it electronic listening or viewing devices or by psychological tests. And with one or two exceptions, the Congress and employers share the public's concern.

Employers should recognize that they are going to have to improve "face-to-face" techniques for improving productivity, reducing pilferage and the like and not count on electronic devices and more "intrusive" employee tests to do the job for them.

Table 3-2			**Whether Various Practices Employed By Business Should Be Illegal: Public and Leaders**	
Question			I will read you some practices that have been used by business organizations for different reasons. For each I would like you to tell me whether they should or should not be forbidden by law. Please think of most jobs in business and government and not jobs which require security clearances or special moral qualities.	

	Public		Leaders	
		Full-Time	Business	
	Total	Employed	Employers	Congress
(Number of respondents)	(1,506)	(612)	(200)	(77)
Listening in on the conversations of employees to find out what they think about their supervisors and managers				
Should be forbidden	83%	84%	70%	77%
Should not be forbidden	14%	14%	28%	18%
Not sure	3%	2%	3%	5%
Installing closed circuit television to obtain continuous checks on how fast workers perform				
Should be forbidden	66%	69%	45%	34%
Should not be forbidden	28%	27%	51%	60%
Not sure	5%	4%	4%	6%
Asking a job applicant to take a lie detector test				
Should be forbidden	62%	65%	55%	60%
Should not be forbidden	31%	30%	42%	38%
Not sure	7%	6%	3%	3%
Asking a job applicant to take a psychological test				
Should be forbidden	48%	50%	25%	45%
Should not be forbidden	40%	40%	69%	49%
Not sure	12%	10%	7%	5%
Requiring an employee to take a lie detector test when there is suspicion of theft in his department				
Should be forbidden	43%	47%	42%	43%
Should not be forbidden	48%	46%	56%	52%
Not sure	9%	7%	3%	5%
Keeping a closed circuit television watch on the work or sales floor to prevent theft and pilfering by employees				
Should be forbidden	42%	43%	20%	18%
Should not be forbidden	52%	51%	77%	77%
Not sure	6%	6%	4%	5%

35

Privacy

3. Findings	***Confidence In Employers Treating Personal Information Properly***

The public generally believes that employers treat their employees' personal information fairly.

Over three-quarters (76%) believe it is not at all likely that their employers have ever released information from their personal life improperly.

And fully 83% do not know of any occasion when their employers have used personal information about their employees unfairly.

Table 3-3

Likelihood of Employer Having Improperly Released Contents of Personnel File: Public
(Base: Full-time employees)

Question

How likely do you think it is that your employer has ever released any information from your personnel file improperly—very likely, somewhat likely, or not at all likely?

	Full-Time
(Number of respondents)	Employed (603)
Very likely	7%
Somewhat likely	13%
Not at all likely	76%
Not sure	4%

Table 3-4

Whether Employer Ever Used Personal Employee Information Unfairly: Public
(Base: Full-time employees)

Question

Do you know of any occasion when your employer used personal information about employees unfairly?

	Full-Time
(Number of respondents)	Employed (599)
Yes, know of occasion	14%
No, don't know of occasion	83%
Not sure	2%

Further, most employees seem to feel that the information contained in their personal files is accurate, up-to-date, and fair. Large majorities of employees say they have never been turned down for a job or for a promotion because of information that was inaccurate (86%), out-of-date (89%), or unfair (84%).

Table 3-5	**Whether Have Been Refused a Job or Promotion Due to Inaccurate, Out-Of-Date, or Unfair Information: Public**

Question	Have you ever been turned down for a job or for a promotion because of information about you which you felt was inaccurate/out-of-date/unfair?

	Total Public	Full-Time Employed
(Number of respondents)	(1,502)	(611)
Inaccurate		
Yes	10%	11%
No	88%	86%
Not sure	3%	3%
Out-of-date		
Yes	7%	7%
No	89%	89%
Not sure	3%	4%
Unfair		
Yes	13%	14%
No	84%	83%
Not sure	3%	3%

4. Findings

Employee Sensitivity About Salaries and Health Insurance Claims

Employees do not appear to be overly concerned that their salaries or health claims might be revealed.

Almost seven in 10 employees (69%) would not be upset if fellow employees knew their salary.

Table 3-6	**Whether Would Be Upset If Employees' Salaries Were Released: Public** (Base: Full-time employees)

Question	How upset would you be if everybody at work knew how much you and all the other employees are paid—very upset, somewhat upset, or not at all upset?

	Full-Time Employed
(Number of respondents)	(601)
Very upset	14%
Somewhat upset	16%
Not at all upset	69%
Not sure	2%

*Fully 81% of employees are not too concerned that their supervisor or some other member of management will see their health and medical claims before they are sent to the insurance company. Indeed, 95% of employees say they have never **not** submitted a health insurance claim because they did not want their employer or other employees to know the details of the claim.*

Privacy

Table 3-7	**Degree of Concern Over Management Seeing Insurance Claims: Public** *(Base: Full-time employees)*
Question	How concerned are you that your supervisor or some other member of management in your company will see your health and medical insurance claims before they are sent to the insurance company—very concerned, somewhat concerned, not too concerned, or not concerned at all?

	Full-Time Employed
(Number of respondents)	*(598)*
Very concerned	9%
Somewhat concerned	9%
Not too concerned	22%
Not at all concerned	59%
Not sure	1%

Table 3-8	**Whether Have Not Submitted Insurance Claim Because Wanted the Details to Remain Private: Public** *(Base: Full-time employees)*
Question	Have you ever **not** submitted a health insurance claim at your workplace because you did not want your employer or other employees to know the details of the claim and treatment you received?

	Full-Time Employed
(Number of respondents	*(603)*
Yes, has happened	4%
No, has not happened	95%
Not sure	1%

5. Findings	**The Right to Review and Question Information in Employee File**

Even though employees are relatively confident that employers treat personal information responsibly, nevertheless, employees strongly believe they should have the right to look at and question supervisors' reports to management on their promotability (88%) and employers' formal job performance review (88%). Two-thirds (65%) also want the right to look at and question the personal notes supervisors keep about employees' performance.

Employers and members of Congress generally agree with employees on these issues with one exception—53% of employers and 70% of Congress do not feel employees should be able to review and question their supervisors' personal notes on their job performance.

	Public		Leaders	
	Total	Full-Time Employed	Business Employers	Congress
Table 3-9				

Whether Employees Should Have the Right to Look at Information Employers Maintain on Them: Public and Leaders

Question	*I am going to read to you some of the kinds of information that employers keep on their employees. I would like you to tell me whether an employee should, or should not, have a right to look at and question each kind of information.*

	Public		Leaders	
		Full-Time Employed	*Business Employers*	*Congress*
	Total			
(Number of respondents)	*(1,508)*	*(611)*	*(200)*	*(77)*
Supervisor's reports to management as to whether the employee is suitable for promotion				
Should have the right	86%	88%	74%	65%
Should not have the right	10%	9%	26%	29%
Not sure	4%	4%	1%	6%
Employer's formal job performance review of the employee				
Should have the right	86%	88%	95%	83%
Should not have the right	10%	9%	5%	14%
Not sure	4%	2%	–	3%
The personal notes a supervisor keeps about the employee's performance				
Should have the right	64%	65%	46%	30%
Should not have the right	30%	31%	53%	70%
Not sure	6%	4%	2%	–

6. Findings	**The Need for Communication Between Employers and Employees**

Despite the fact that most employees do not feel overly sensitive about other employees knowing their health problems or their salary, 83% feel it is "very important" than an employer should inform an employee before releasing any personal information from their files, except for regular reporting of information required by law.

Moreover, 42% of employees think that all employers should have a specific policy designed to safeguard employees' personal information.

Observation	*We see further evidence here that the public is concerned about the potential for the abuse of their personal information. They want a formal mechanism to ward off that potential abuse.*	*Corporations would do well to follow the lead of the few companies that have developed and communicated formal corporate privacy policies.*

Table 3-10	**Importance of Employer Informing of the Release of Personal Information: Public and Leaders**

Question	How important do you think it is that an employer should inform employees before releasing any personal information from employment files, except the regular reporting required by law—very important, somewhat important, or not important at all?

	Public		Leaders	
		Full-Time	Business	
	Total	Employed	Employers	Congress
(Number of respondents)	(1,508)	(611)	(199)	(77)
Very important	83%	85%	84%	94%
Somewhat important	12%	13%	12%	5%
Not at all important	3%	2%	3%	–
Not sure	1%	*	2%	1%

*Less than 0.5%

Table 3-11	**Whether Employers Should Have Policy to Safeguard Employees' Personnel and Medical Files: Public and Leaders**

Question	Do you think that all employers should have a specific company policy designed to safeguard the information contained in their employees' personnel and medical files?

	Public		Leaders	
		Full-Time	Business	
	Total	Employed	Employers	Congress
(Number of respondents)	(1,509)	(611)	(200)	(77)
Should have policy	92%	93%	96%	97%
Should not have policy	4%	5%	3%	1%
Not sure	4%	3%	1%	1%

7. Findings

The Need for a Law to Determine Employee Access to Personnel Files

Although employers and employees basically agree that employees should have access to their personnel files, they disagree sharply about the need for a law to enforce these rights.

Seventy percent of employees feel that employers should not be allowed to determine what these rights are and think that a law should be passed to specify those rights. However, 64% of employers feel these rights should be determined by employers. The Congressional respondents are divided, with 48% feeling the rights should be decided by the employer and 44% feeling that a law is necessary.

Observation

Even though most employees feel their employers have not invaded their privacy, they insist on the fail-safe mechanism of the law.

| | **Table 3-12** | | **Whether Employers or Law Should Determine Employee Rights Regarding Access to Personal Files: Public and Leaders** |

Table 3-12   **Whether Employers or Law Should Determine Employee Rights Regarding Access to Personal Files: Public and Leaders**

Question   *Do you think employers should decide what rights employees have regarding access to their personnel files or do you think a law should be passed to specify these rights?*

	Public		Leaders	
(Number of respondents)	*Total* (1,506)	*Full-Time Employed* (609)	*Business Employers* (200)	*Congress* (77)
A law should be passed	65%	70%	33%	44%
Left to employers	25%	23%	64%	48%
Not sure	9%	7%	3%	8%

8. Findings   **The Need For A Law That Requires Employers to Reveal Any Information Which Shows That Health May Be Affected By Work Conditions**

Finally, it should be noted that employees are overwhelmingly in favor of a law which would require employers to inform them of any information they might have which shows that their health is being affected by conditions at work.

Table 3-13   **Whether There Should Be A Law Requiring Employers To Inform Employees That Their Health Is Being Affected By Conditions At The Workplace: Public And Leaders**

Question   *If employers have any information that the health of employees is being affected by conditions at work, do you think they should or should not be required by law to inform all employees concerned?*

	Public		Leaders	
(Number of respondents)	*Total* (1,499)	*Full-Time Employed* (608)	*Business Employers* (200)	*Congress* (77)
Should be required by law	91%	91%	84%	87%
Should not be required	5%	7%	14%	10%
Not sure	3%	2%	2%	3%

Chapter 4

*The Privacy
Intensive Industries:*

Credit

Privacy

Objectives	The issue of individual privacy as it relates to the credit area can be analyzed on the same dimensions that the employment area was. There are three key aspects—the intrusiveness of information gathering, the degree to which information already collected is kept confidential, and the right of the consumer to have access to his credit files.

1. Findings	**Intrusiveness of Credit Institutions Relative to Other Organizations**
	Earlier it was found that credit institutions were among the most highly criticized by the public for their intrusiveness and for their improper sharing of the information they collect. Particularly noteworthy is the divergence between the views of the executives in the credit industry on the one hand, and those of the public, and, most importantly, of the Congressional respondents and federal regulators on the other hand. While the executives in the credit industry do not feel that they ask for too much information in order to give credit, substantial percentages of the public, Congressional respondents, and federal regulators disagree.

Table 4-1	**Whether Organizations Ask For Too Much Personal Information: Public And Leaders**
Question	I am going to read you a list of organizations and individuals which sometimes collect or use information about us. For each of these I would like you to tell me whether you feel they limit their personal information about individuals to what is really necessary or whether they ask for too much personal information.

			Leaders				
			Privacy Intensive Industries			Government Officials	
(Number of respondents)	Total Public (1,511)	Rank Among 18 Organizations	Credit (32)	Credit Card (40)	Banks (36)	Congress (77)	Regulatory Officials (53)
Finance companies		(1)					
Ask for too much	45%		16%	20%	3%	60%	51%
Limit their demands	33%		72%	78%	92%	25%	26%
Not sure	22%		13%	3%	6%	16%	23%
Credit bureaus		(2)					
Ask for too much	44%		19%	13%	8%	61%	55%
Limit their demands	31%		75%	88%	89%	22%	13%
Not sure	25%		6%	–	3%	17%	32%
Credit card companies		(5)					
Ask for too much	37%		6%	8%	3%	40%	38%
Limit their demands	46%		94%	93%	94%	55%	55%
Not sure	17%		–	–	3%	5%	8%
Banks		(10)					
Ask for too much	29%		3%	10%	–	35%	36%
Limit their demands	63%		97%	90%	100%	62%	57%
Not sure	8%		–	–	–	3%	8%

2. Findings	**Whether Improper Information Asked for on Credit Applications**
	While credit granting institutions are among the most criticized, only 24% of the public feel they have been asked to supply information they felt was either improper or unnecessary.
	Asked what that information was, income (18%), credit references (15%), employment (11%) and assets (10%) were the most frequently mentioned.

There can be no doubt about the sharp conflict between the needs of the credit industry—as perceived by its leaders—and the views of the public as to what is proper. Both may have to compromise if conflict is to be avoided. Some of the replies of the public—i.e. that it is improper to ask for income—are naive. However, it would be a grave mistake to think education and communication alone will resolve the conflict.

Table 4-2   **Whether Improper Information Requested When Applying For Credit: Public And Leaders**

Question   Now I'd like to ask you some questions about different types of **institutions that give people credit such as banks, credit card companies, and stores.** Have you ever been asked to supply information that you felt was improper or unnecessary when applying for any type of credit?

	(Number Of Respondents)	Yes	No	Not Sure
Total Public	**(1,499)**	**24%**	**72%**	**3%**
Age				
18–29 years	(421)	28%	68%	3%
30–49 years	(556)	33%	64%	3%
50 and over	(516)	13%	83%	4%
Education				
8th grade or less	(136)	13%	82%	3%
High school	(743)	23%	72%	4%
College	(610)	28%	68%	2%
Income				
Under $7,000	(278)	16%	79%	4%
$7,000–$14,999	(417)	24%	73%	3%
$15,000–$24,999	(488)	28%	67%	4%
$25,000 and over	(229)	29%	69%	1%
Political Philosophy				
Conservative	(482)	23%	74%	3%
Middle-of-the-road	(564)	23%	73%	3%
Liberal	(262)	36%	60%	3%
Leaders				
Privacy Intensive Industry				
Credit	(32)	22%	78%	–
Credit Card	(40)	25%	75%	–
Banks	(36)	11%	89%	–
Government Officials				
Congress	(77)	31%	65%	4%
Regulatory officials	(53)	58%	42%	–

Privacy

Table 4-3   **Improper Information Requested When Applying For Credit: Public and Leaders**

(Base: Have been asked improper or unnecessary information)

Question   *What kind of information was that?*

		Leaders				
		Privacy Intensive Industries			Government Officials	
(Number of respondents)	Total Public (373)	Credit (6)	Credit Card (10)	Banks (4)	Congress (22)	Regulatory Officials (30)
Income, salary, earnings	18%	33%	40%	50%	14%	13%
Questions about personal life not related to credit rating (e.g., drinking habits, politics)	17%	–	–	–	14%	10%
Family life, home environment	15%	17%	10%	25%	32%	23%
Credit reference, ratings; money owed, outstanding bills	15%	–	–	–	9%	10%
Marital status	14%	–	20%	–	9%	30%
Unfair questions about job, employment	11%	17%	–	–	18%	13%
Value of assets, property	10%	17%	10%	–	9%	13%
Finances; money in bank accounts	7%	–	10%	25%	–	7%
Questions relating to spouse	6%	17%	–	–	18%	23%
Age	6%	17%	10%	–	5%	7%
Where you live and for how long	5%	–	10%	50%	36%	7%
Whether you rent or own home	5%	–	10%	–	18%	13%
References; cosigners	5%	33%	–	–	5%	3%
Unfair restrictions regarding a woman's obtaining credit	5%	17%	–	–	–	3%
Sex	4%	–	–	–	5%	3%
Information about relatives financial and credit status	3%	17%	–	–	–	–
Whether you have ever been in jail or arrested	3%	–	–	–	–	–
Race	2%	–	–	–	5%	7%
Other sources of income	*	–	–	25%	–	–
Social security number	–	–	–	–	–	10%
Educational background	–	17%	–	–	5%	3%
Any other answer	8%	–	10%	–	–	7%
Not sure	8%	–	20%	–	–	3%

*Less than 0.5%

3. Findings	**Why Consumers Believe They Are Refused Credit**

About one in four consumers say he/she has been refused credit. Over half of those who have been refused feel it was based on unfair information, half believe the decision was based on incomplete information and a little over a third believe it was based on inaccurate information.

Table 4-4	**Whether Have Been Refused Credit: Public**
Question	Have you ever been refused credit?

	Total Public
(Number of respondents)	(1,501)
Have been refused credit	26%
Have not been refused credit	70%
Not sure	1%
No response/refused	2%

Table 4-5	**Reason For Being Refused Credit: Public**
	(Base: Have been refused credit)
Question	Do you believe the decision to refuse you credit was based on information which was inaccurate/unfair/incomplete?

	Total Public
(Number of respondents)	(394)
Inaccurate	
Believe	38%
Do not believe	50%
Not sure	11%
Unfair	
Believe	63%
Do not believe	30%
Not sure	7%
Incomplete	
Believe	51%
Do not believe	40%
Not sure	9%

4. Findings	**Awareness of the Fair Credit Reporting Act**

The importance of individual access to credit records was recognized in the Fair Credit Reporting Act, which gives the individual the right to see his credit file when he has been refused credit. However, the survey reveals that only 56% of Americans are aware of this right. While this is a majority it still leaves 44% of Americans who are not aware that they have this right.

Table 4-6	**Do You Have the Right to See Credit Bureau Report: Public**
Question	Do you know whether you have the legal right to see any credit bureau report that might be used in a decision to deny you credit, insurance, or employment, or not?

	Total Public
(Number of respondents)	(1,502)
Do have the right	56%
Do not have the right	13%
Not sure	31%

Chapter 5

Privacy

Objectives

The insurance industry collects detailed information about millions of people every year who apply for homeowners insurance, auto insurance, and life insurance. This chapter examines two key aspects of this activity—the extent to which the insurance companies are perceived to seek more information than is necessary or desirable, and the extent to which the insurance industry is thought to be misusing the information they collect.

1. Findings

Perceptions of the Insurance Industry Compared to Other Industries

Thirty-eight percent of the American people feel that insurance companies collect too much personal information. Insurance companies rank third after finance companies and credit bureaus in this regard.

The replies of the various leadership groups to this question vary dramatically—from the 61% of state insurance commissioners who believe that insurance companies ask for too much information to the mere 3% of bank executives who feel this way. The greater majority of business employers and those in privacy intensive industries are not concerned about the intrusiveness of the insurance industry. But there is a high level of concern, not only among the state insurance commissioners, but among regulatory officials and Congressional respondents.

Observation

Insurance companies had better pay heed, since not only do consumers rank them high among industries that ask for too much information, but also a majority of the state insurance commissioners who regulate the industry feel this way.

Clearly insurance companies will have to take a hard look at the information they ask for—and sooner rather than later.

Table 5-1

Whether Insurance Companies Ask For Too Much Personal Information: Public and Leaders

Question

I am going to read you a list of organizations and individuals which sometimes collect or use information about us. For each of these I would like you to tell me whether you feel they limit their personal information about individuals to what is really necessary or whether they ask for too much personal information.

	(Number Of Respondents)	Insurance Companies		
		Ask For Too Much	Limit Their Demands	Not Sure
Total Public	**(1,511)**	**38%**	**54%**	**9%**
Leaders				
Business employers	(200)	27%	71%	2%
Privacy Intensive Industry				
Credit	(32)	13%	88%	–
Credit card	(40)	23%	73%	5%
Banks	(36)	3%	92%	6%
Insurance	(36)	17%	83%	–
Computer	(36)	39%	61%	–
Government Officials				
State insurance commissioners	(33)	61%	36%	3%
Congress	(77)	47%	48%	5%
Law enforcement officials	(42)	24%	71%	5%
Regulatory officials	(53)	49%	42%	9%
Doctors	(33)	42%	55%	3%

2. Findings

What Information Should be Collected for Life Insurance and Health Insurance

Large majorities of the American people feel that insurance companies should not ask for information about the applicant's lifestyle, moral character, income, or criminal record, if any. Furthermore, sizable majorities even feel that it is wrong for the insurance industry to collect information such as whether the applicant already has life or health insurance, or the details of prior insurance claims made by the applicant.

Sizable majorities, however, do feel that insurance companies should be able to collect many other kinds of information such as the applicant's drinking habits, type of employment, sex, health and medical history.

Majorities of the insurance executives interviewed agreed with the public that they should not be able to collect information on the applicant's life-style or moral character, and fully 44% do not think that they should ask questions about the applicant's criminal record, if any. Apart from these three items, most insurance industry executives feel that they should be able to collect all of the other types of information listed.

The replies of state insurance commissioners and Congressional respondents are very different from those of insurance executives. Both the insurance commissioners and those in Congress oppose the collection of most types of information that some insurance companies use to decide whether or not to issue life and health insurance policies.

Observation

While the survey does not explore the reasons why people oppose the collection of these data, it seems likely that many people do not understand the reasons insurance companies ask for them. A tentative conclusion, based on the data discussed above, is that the insurance industry must do a much better job of communicating the reasons why information is collected if they are to avoid more rigorous controls.

Table 5-2

Types of Information Insurance Companies Should Not Have Right to Collect: Public and Leaders

Question

*I am going to read to you a list of the types of information which insurance companies may use to decide whether or not to give people **life insurance** or **health and medical insurance,** and what premiums to charge. Please say for each one whether you think insurance companies should or should not have the right to obtain this information.*

Privacy

(Number of respondents)	Total Public (1,502)	Insurance Industry (36)	State Insurance Commis-sioners (33)	Congress (77)
Should not have the right				
Information on the applicant's lifestyle	77%	58%	73%	84%
The applicant's moral character	71%	53%	76%	84%
The applicant's income	70%	22%	55%	61%
What other health or life insurance the applicant already has	63%	8%	24%	45%
The applicant's criminal record, if any	60%	44%	48%	73%
Information relating to claims the applicant has made to other insurance companies	55%	17%	42%	44%
Whether the applicant has been turned down or rated a bad risk for health or life insurance	44%	22%	45%	40%
Whether the applicant smokes, or not	41%	17%	15%	14%
Whether or not the applicant engages in sports activities which involve some real physical risk	39%	14%	21%	22%
The applicant's drinking habits	34%	11%	24%	31%
The applicant's type of employment	32%	6%	12%	16%
The applicant's sex	25%	19%	15%	23%
The applicant's health and medical history	10%	3%	3%	4%
The applicant's age	10%	3%	6%	5%

3. Findings

What Information Should be Collected for Automobile Insurance

Majorities of the American people oppose the collection of data about the applicant's moral character, credit-worthiness, length of residence at his or her present address, and former claims made to other insurance companies. And sizable minorities oppose the collection of many other kinds of information.

The replies of insurance executives concerning the collection of many of these kinds of information are remarkably similar to those of the American people. However, they strongly differ with the public on one item—insurance executives overwhelmingly support the collection of information relating to other insurance claims. In addition, they feel it is proper to inquire about the applicant's drinking habits, the driving record of others who will be using the car, and the type of car driven.

Majorities of both state insurance commissioners and Congressmen and their aides oppose the collection of information about an applicant's moral character, credit-worthiness, and length of residence at his or her present address, but they are much more sympathetic than the general public toward the insurance industry's need to collect information about the applicant's other claims, the use that will be made of the car, the driving records of others who will be using the car, and the type of car. The replies of government officials diverge most sharply from those of most insurance executives on the collection of information about the applicant's type of employment and drinking habits.

Table 5-3

Types of Information Insurance Companies Should Not Have Right to Collect: Public and Leaders

Question

*I am going to read to you a list of the types of information which insurance companies may use to decide whether or not to sell people **automobile insurance** and what premiums to charge. Please say for each one whether you think insurance companies should or should not have the right to obtain this information.*

(Number of respondents)	Total Public (1,511)	Leaders		
		Insurance Industry (36)	State Insurance Commis- sioners (33)	Congress (77)
Should not have right to information on:				
The applicant's moral character	71%	67%	82%	88%
The applicant's credit-worthiness and his ability to pay his bills	53%	53%	70%	53%
How long the applicant has lived at his or her present address	53%	53%	70%	58%
Information relating to claims the applicant has made to other insurance companies	51%	17%	27%	34%
The applicant's criminal record, if any	48%	39%	48%	57%
The applicant's type of employment	45%	31%	55%	45%
The applicant's sex	34%	36%	39%	47%
The applicant's health and medical history	34%	33%	24%	39%
The applicant's drinking habits	30%	19%	36%	49%
The use that will be made of the car	27%	6%	6%	6%
The driving record of others who will be using the car	19%	3%	3%	6%
The type of car driven	18%	3%	6%	5%
The applicant's age	13%	11%	12%	14%
The applicant's driving record	7%	–	–	–

4. Findings	**Reaction to One Proposal to Reduce the Cost of Automobile Insurance** *By way of a "trade-off", the overwhelming majority of people would be prepared to allow the insurance companies to inspect the mileage indicator on their car twice a year if it meant a savings to them of $50 per year in the cost of their auto insurance.*
Observation	*Here we see solid evidence that the public is willing to "trade-off" certain invasions of privacy in return for value.* *The insurance industry might profitably explore other such "trade-offs."*
Table 5-4	**Willingness to Allow Inspection of Mileage Indicator to Save on Cost of Auto Insurance: Public**
Question	*If it would mean a savings to you for $50 per year in the cost of your auto insurance, would you be willing to let your insurance company inspect your car's mileage indicator twice a year, or not?*

	Total Public
(Number of respondents)	(1,498)
Yes, would be willing	73%
No, would not be willing	17%
Not applicable, don't have a car	7%
Not sure	3%

5. Findings	**Courses of Action Insurance Companies Might Pursue to Evaluate Insurability** *Strong majorities of the American people oppose the investigation of an applicant for health insurance to see if he or she is frequenting dangerous bars or sections of*

Privacy

town (which clearly are a worse insurance risk), the checking of the contents of an applicant's home to see what would be covered by a homeowners policy, and the use of a central computer to find out if an applicant was ever turned down for life or health insurance.

The views of most people are supported by large majorities of those in Congress and state insurance commissioners, while majorities of insurance executives agree with the public on two out of the three issues. (The one exception is that most insurance executives approve the use of a central computer file to find out whether an applicant was ever turned down for life or health insurance).

Table 5-5	**Three Things Insurance Companies Should Not Do: Public and Leaders**
Question	I will read you three things insurance companies could do to find out whether or not someone is a good risk for insurance. Please say for each one whether you feel it should or should not be allowed.

| | | Leaders | | |
	Total Public (1,508)	Insurance Industry (36)	State Insurance Commissioners (33)	Congress (77)
(Number of respondents)				
Should not be allowed to:				
Investigate an applicant's personal life to see if he or she is frequenting dangerous bars or sections of town	85%	69%	79%	91%
Have someone go through an applicant's home and check through its contents to see what would be covered by a homeowners policy	73%	60%	76%	65%
Use a central computer file to find out if an applicant was ever turned down for life or health insurance	68%	33%	52%	64%

6. Findings

Should the Personal Information an Insurance Company Collects be Determined by Law

A sizable majority (65%) of the public feels that the types of information that insurance companies gather about applicants **should** be determined by law. Not surprisingly, insurance industry executives would oppose legislation of this kind by 79–18%.

Replies of state insurance commissioners and Congressional respondents could be important on this question, and a majority of the former and a plurality of the latter favor such legislation.

Table 5-6	**Whether Amount of Personal Information to be Collected Should be Determined by Insurance Companies or by Law: Public and Leaders**
Question	Do you think that insurance companies ought to be allowed to determine what types of personal information they can gather on people in order to decide whether they will give them insurance and what premiums they will charge, or should the types of information they can gather be determined by law?

| | | Leaders | | |
	Total Public (1,491)	Insurance Industry (34)	State Insurance Commissioners (33)	Congress (76)
(Number of respondents)				
Should be determined by law	65%	18%	55%	49%
Insurance companies allowed to determine	27%	79%	39%	47%
Not sure	8%	3%	6%	4%

Observation	The public and the insurance industry are on a collision course over the issue of what information can be properly collected for insurance. It is possible	that the gulf between insurers and the insured could be narrowed if the industry did a better job of explaining why information is collected.

Chapter 6

The Privacy
Intensive Industries:

Doctors And Hospitals

Privacy

| Objectives | The purpose of this section is to examine public and leadership perceptions of private doctors and hospitals in terms of the three measures that have been used in the preceding sections of this report. |

---

1. Findings

Propriety of Information Collected

Doctors are rated the least intrusive of 18 organizations and individuals named in this survey. Table 6-1 shows that a mere 11% of the public feels that doctors ask for too much personal information. Doctors also receive very little criticism from the leadership groups on this measure. The most critical leaders are federal regulators, and their degree of criticism (11%) is no larger than that of the public.

The public is twice as likely to be critical of hospitals than it is of doctors for asking for too much personal information. Indeed, the public considers hospitals (24%) to be as intrusive as local police (23%).

Except for federal regulators (32%), the leadership groups are less critical of hospitals than the public is. However, in varying degrees, all of the leadership groups are more critical of hospitals for asking for too much personal information than they are of doctors.

Table 6-1

Whether Hospitals and Private Doctors Ask for Too Much Personal Information: Public and Leaders

Question

I am going to read you a list of organizations and individuals which sometimes collect or use information about us. For each of these I would like you to tell me whether you feel they limit their personal information about individuals to what is really necessary or whether they ask for too much personal information.

| | | Leaders | | | | | |
| | | Hospitals | | | Private Doctors | | |
	(Number Of Respondents)	Ask For Too Much	Limit Their Demands	Not Sure	Ask For Too Much	Limit Their Demands	Not Sure
Total Public	**(1,510)**	**24%**	**69%**	**6%**	**11%**	**84%**	**5%**
Leaders							
Business employers	(200)	17%	81%	2%	3%	97%	1%
Privacy Intensive Industry							
Credit	(32)	16%	78%	6%	–	97%	3%
Credit card	(40)	5%	95%	–	–	100%	–
Banks	(36)	3%	97%	–	–	97%	3%
Insurance	(36)	11%	89%	–	3%	94%	3%
Computer	(36)	17%	78%	6%	6%	92±%	3%
Government Officials							
State insurance commissioners	(33)	18%	76%	6%	3%	94%	3%
Congress	(77)	19%	70%	10%	9%	83%	8%
Law enforcement officials	(42)	14%	83%	2%	7%	90%	2%
Regulatory officials	(53)	32%	57%	11%	11%	79%	9%
Doctors	(33)	21%	73%	6%	9%	91%	–

2. Findings

Confidentiality of Information Collected

Doctors are the least criticized of 18 organizations and individuals for their efforts to keep personal information they possess on patients confidential. Only 17% of the public feels that doctors should be doing more in this regard. Notably, doctors (30%) are almost twice as likely as the public to feel that they should be doing more to keep medical records confidential.

Hospitals are also one of the least criticized organizations on the measure of confidentiality. While 23% of the public feels hospitals should be doing more to keep records confidential, only the telephone company (22%) and private doctors (17%) receive better ratings. All of the leadership groups, excluding bank executives and executives in the insurance industry, are more critical of hospitals than they are of doctors. Among the leadership groups, doctors are the most critical of hospitals and 39% feel hospitals should be doing more to keep patient records confidential.

Table 6-2

Whether Hospitals and Private Doctors Should be Doing More to Maintain Confidentiality of Personal Information: Public and Leaders

Question

Now I'm going to read you the same list of organizations again. This time I would like you to tell me whether each organization is currently doing enough to keep the personal information they have on individuals confidential, or should they be doing more?

		Leaders					
		Hospitals			Private Doctors		
	(Number Of Respondents)	Should Be Doing More	Doing Enough	Not Sure	Should Be Doing More	Doing Enough	Not Sure
Total Public	**(1,504)**	**23%**	**66%**	**11%**	**17%**	**75%**	**8%**
Leaders							
Business employers	(200)	19%	75%	7%	13%	82%	6%
Privacy Intensive Industry							
Credit	(32)	13%	81%	6%	9%	84%	6%
Credit card	(40)	10%	90%	–	3%	95%	3%
Banks	(36)	6%	89%	6%	8%	86%	6%
Insurance	(36)	11%	78%	11%	17%	81%	3%
Computer	(36)	29%	63%	9%	14%	77%	9%
Government Officials							
State insurance commissioners	(32)	31%	63%	6%	19%	75%	6%
Congress	(77)	26%	60%	14%	21%	74%	5%
Law enforcement officials	(42)	15%	80%	5%	10%	85%	5%
Regulatory officials	(52)	30%	52%	18%	18%	64%	18%
Doctors	(33)	39%	61%	–	30%	70%	–

Privacy

3. Findings

Access To Medical Records

There is a consensus among the public, Congressional respondents, business employers, and regulatory officials that people should have the legal right to see their medical records, whether held by their personal doctor or a hospital. Doctors and executives in the insurance industry are slightly more reluctant to agree that people should have this legal right. Nevertheless, majorities of both groups feel the public should have the legal right to see its records.

Table 6-3

Whether People Should Have Access to Medical Records: Public and Leaders

Question

Now I'd like to ask you some questions about doctors and hospitals. Do you think people who want to should have the legal right to see their medical records held by their personal doctor/a clinic or hospital, or not?

		Leaders				
(Number of respondents)	Total Public (1,509)	Business Employers (200)	Insurance Industry (36)	Congress (77)	Regulatory Officials (53)	Doctors (33)
Their personal doctor						
Should have the right	91%	89%	75%	94%	91%	64%
Should not have the right	8%	11%	14%	4%	2%	36%
Not sure	1%	–	11%	3%	8%	–
Clinic or hospital						
Should have the right	91%	90%	78%	92%	91%	64%
Should not have the right	7%	10%	14%	4%	2%	36%
Not sure	2%	–	8%	4%	8%	–

Overwhelming majorities of all respondents feel that if they were being treated by a doctor, they would want to know all the relevant information about their illness even though they might be told they were dying.

Table 6-4

Whether Would Want To Be Told You Are Dying: Public And Leaders

Question

If you were being treated by a doctor, would you want your doctor to tell you all the relevant information about your illness even though you might be told that you were dying?

	(Number Of Respondents)	Would Want To Be Told	Would Not Want To Be Told	Not Sure
Total Public	**(1,508)**	**87%**	**7%**	**6%**
Leaders				
Business employers	(200)	95%	2%	3%
Insurance industry	(36)	94%	6%	–
Congress	(77)	100%	–	–
Regulatory officials	(53)	92%	2%	6%
Doctors	(33)	91%	9%	–

Observation

Although only small minorities are critical of doctors or hospitals, the overwhelming majority want access to their medical records—perhaps as a fail-safe.

Chapter 7

Privacy

Objectives	*This chapter explores two dimensions of the problem of personal privacy closely related to the news media—making public certain types of information it gathers on people for a news story, and the courts' rights of access to a journalist's notes and sources.*

1. Findings	**Whether the News Media Asks for Too Much Personal Information**
	It was noted earlier that while only one in three Americans (31%) feel that the news media ask for too much personal information, a large majority of most of the leadership groups (except those in the computer industry) are highly critical of the fact that the news media asks for too much personal information. The two most critical groups are bank executives and law enforcement officials; 78% of both groups feel that the news media ask for too much personal information. The least critical leaders are the federal regulators (58%).
Table 7-1	**Whether the News Media Ask for Too Much Personal Information: Public and Leaders**
Question	*I am going to read you a list of organizations and individuals which sometimes collect or use information about us. For each of these I would like you to tell me whether you feel they limit their personal information about individuals to what is really necessary or whether they ask for too much personal information.*

		Newspapers, Magazines, And Television		
	(Number Of Respondents)	*Ask For Too Much*	*Limit Their Demands*	*Not Sure*
Total Public	**(1,510)**	**31%**	**45%**	**24%**
Leaders				
Business employers	*(200)*	69%	22%	9%
Privacy Intensive Industry				
Credit	*(32)*	75%	22%	3%
Credit card	*(40)*	65%	30%	5%
Banks	*(36)*	78%	14%	8%
Insurance	*(36)*	72%	22%	6%
Computer	*(36)*	42%	36%	22%
Government Officials				
State insurance commissioners	*(33)*	68%	26%	6%
Congress	*(77)*	60%	32%	8%
Law enforcement officials	*(42)*	78%	20%	2%
Regulatory officials	*(53)*	58%	25%	17%
Doctors	*(33)*	61%	36%	3%

2. Findings	**News Media Practices That Constitute an Invasion of Privacy**
	Large majorities of both the public and leadership groups feel that the publication of the following items **would be** *an invasion of privacy:*

* *The details of an extramarital affair that a public official is having with another person.*

* *The names of people on welfare.*

* *A photograph of a well-known politician entering a pornographic book store.*

With one notable exception, majorities of both the public and leadership groups feel the publication of the following items **would not** *be an invasion of privacy:*

* *The names of doctors who have received large sums of money under Medicare and Medicaid.*

* *The names of people who are arrested for possessing illegal drugs.*

* *The contents of confidential government papers that reveal incompetence or dishonesty by public officials.*

Doctors are the exception here, with 67% believing that the publication of the names of doctors who have received large sums of money under Medicare and Medicaid would be an invasion of privacy.

By a slim 51% to 44% plurality, the public feels that publishing the names of young people under 16 years old who are accused of committing crimes **is** *an invasion of privacy. Except for law enforcement officials,majorities or pluralities of the leadership groups* **do** *feel the publication of such information is an invasion of privacy.*

Finally, the public is divided (49%–47%) on the question of whether publishing the names of men who have been arrested for soliciting prostitutes is an invasion of privacy. Slight majorities of business employers (51%), regulatory officials (51%), Congressional respondents (52%), and a large majority of doctors (72%), feel that the publication of this information is an invasion of privacy.

Table 7-2	**Is the Publishing by a Newspaper of Various Types of Information an Invasion of Privacy: Public and Leaders**
Question	*And now some questions about newspapers and television. I am going to read you a list of different types of information that a newspaper might have. For each I would like you to tell me whether you would consider the publishing of this information to be an invasion of privacy or not.*

Privacy

			Privacy Intensive Industries					Government Officials				
Table 7·2												*Leaders*
(Number of respondents)	Total Public (1,513)	Business Employers (200)	Credit (32)	Credit Card (40)	Banks (36)	Insur- ance (36)	Com- puter (36)	State Insurance Commis- sioners (33)	Congress (77)	Law Enforce- ment Offi- cials (42)	Regu- latory Offi- cials (53)	Doctors (33)
	%	%	%	%	%	%	%	%	%	%	%	%
The details of an extramarital affair that a public official is having with another person												
Invasion of privacy	78	69	66	73	61	64	67	82	73	71	79	82
Not an invasion of privacy	19	30	34	28	36	31	33	18	23	19	21	18
Not sure	3	2	–	–	3	6	–	–	4	10	–	–
The names of people on welfare												
Invasion of privacy	71	77	84	83	81	81	58	70	75	71	91	91
Not an invasion of privacy	25	22	16	15	19	19	33	24	23	24	9	9
Not sure	4	2	–	3	–	–	8	6	1	5	–	–
A photograph of a well-known politician entering a pornographic book shop												
Invasion of privacy	70	67	66	68	69	75	53	67	57	52	64	79
Not an invasion of privacy	26	33	34	33	25	25	42	33	42	45	36	21
Not sure	4	1	–	–	6	–	6	–	1	2	–	–
The names of young people under 16 years old who are accused of committing crimes												
Invasion of privacy	51	52	50	60	64	56	64	48	61	45	70	64
Not an invasion of privacy	44	44	38	38	33	44	36	36	35	52	25	33
Not sure	5	5	13	3	3	–	–	15	4	2	6	3
The names of men who have been arrested for soliciting prostitutes												
Invasion of privacy	49	51	41	40	36	50	46	33	52	32	51	72
Not an invasion of privacy	47	49	59	58	64	47	54	67	43	63	45	28
Not sure	4	1	–	3	–	3	–	–	5	5	4	–
The names of doctors who have received large sums of money under Medicare and Medicaid												
Invasion of privacy	30	39	47	33	33	25	33	30	25	21	19	67
Not an invasion of privacy	65	60	53	65	64	75	67	67	74	74	75	33
Not sure	6	2	–	3	3	–	–	3	1	5	6	–
The names of people who are arrested for possessing illegal drugs												
Invasion of privacy	27	27	25	18	25	25	17	18	25	19	42	30
Not an invasion of privacy	68	71	72	83	75	75	83	76	70	79	57	70
Not sure	4	3	3	–	–	–	–	6	5	2	2	–
The contents of confidential government papers that reveal incompetence or dishonesty by public officials												
Invasion of privacy	21	25	25	18	28	33	19	18	13	24	15	21
Not an invasion of privacy	73	71	72	80	69	64	72	70	83	73	77	79
Not sure	6	5	3	3	3	3	8	12	4	2	8	–

By a 73–21% majority, the public rejects the argument that the publication of the contents of confidential government papers that reveal incompetence or dishonesty by public officials is an invasion of privacy. Large majorities of Congressional respondents (83%), law enforcement officials (73%), and regulatory officials (77%) feel similarly.

Table 7-3   **Whether Publishing Contents of Certain Government Papers is an Invasion of Privacy: Public and Leaders**

Question   *And now some questions about newspapers and television. I am going to read you a list of different types of information that a newspaper might have. For each I would like you to tell me whether you would consider the publishing of this information to be an invasion of privacy or not.*

		Leaders		
		Government Officials		
	Total Public	Congress	Law Enforcement Officials	Regulatory Officials
(Number of respondents)	(1,513)	(77)	(42)	(53)
The contents of confidential government papers that reveal incompetence or dishonesty by public officials				
Invasion of privacy	21%	13%	24%	15%
Not an invasion of privacy	73%	83%	73%	77%
Not sure	6%	4%	2%	8%

However, when the same respondents are asked whether they believe that the government should have the right to prosecute anyone who publishes secret materials, 70% of the public and 74% of the law enforcement officials say they favor this right.

Observation   Attitudes to specific instances involving the publication of classified material will depend on whether the public feels that publication damages the national interest or merely exposes dishonesty or corruption in government.

Table 7-4   **Should Government Have the Right to Prosecute Publisher of Secret Materials: Public and Leaders**

Question   *I will read you a few suggestions that people have made. For each, tell me if you would favor strongly, favor somewhat, oppose somewhat, or oppose strongly such a step being taken.*

		Leaders		
		Government Officials		
	Total Public	Congress	Law Enforcement Officials	Regulatory Officials
(Number of respondents)	(1,512)	(77)	(42)	(53)
The government should have the right to prosecute anyone who publishes materials that it classifies as secret				
Favor strongly	48%	19%	60%	25%
Favor somewhat	22%	36%	14%	21%
Oppose somewhat	12%	13%	19%	21%
Oppose strongly	11%	27%	2%	34%
Not sure	6%	4%	5%	–

Privacy

3. Findings	**The Privacy of a Journalist's Notes and Sources**
	By a 62–25% majority, the public supports the view that the privacy of a journalist's notes and sources should be protected from the courts. Executives in credit card companies, banking and computers, Congressional respondents, regulatory officials, and doctors are of the same opinion. State insurance commissioners and law enforcement officials do not agree with this view; 59% and 67%, respectively, feel that reporters should have to reveal all the evidence needed by the courts to reach fair decisions.
Table 7-5	**Should Journalists' Notes and Sources be Revealed to the Courts: Public and Leaders**
Question	*There has recently been a controversy as to whether or not journalists should have to reveal their unpublished notes and sources to the courts. **One view** is that the privacy of sources should be protected to ensure that people feel free to talk to the press. **Others** say that this is less important than providing the courts with all the evidence needed to reach fair decisions. Which is closest to the way you feel?*

	(Number Of Respondents)	Privacy Of Journalists' Notes And Sources Should Be Protected	They Should Have To Reveal Them To The Courts	Not Sure
Total Public	**(1,505)**	**62%**	**25%**	**13%**
Leaders				
Business employers	(198)	55%	41%	4%
Privacy Intensive Industry				
Credit	(32)	47%	38%	16%
Credit card	(40)	63%	30%	8%
Banks	(36)	53%	39%	8%
Insurance	(35)	49%	37%	14%
Computer	(36)	64%	33%	3%
Government Officials				
State insurance commissioners	(32)	31%	59%	9%
Congress	(77)	58%	30%	12%
Law enforcement officials	(42)	29%	67%	5%
Regulatory officials	(52)	69%	25%	6%
Doctors	(33)	61%	36%	3%

Observation	*The public's position in the current debate about the First Amendment as it relates to the news media is essentially pragmatic rather than ideological. While*	*strongly supportive of the freedom of the press on several key issues, most people believe there are real limits beyond which the press should not go.*

Chapter 8

Privacy

Objectives

One of the most fundamental philosophical questions of the last decade in this country relates to how the government can maintain a proper balance between the need for personal information on its citizens in order to provide services, insure law and order, and provide for national security of the nation on the one hand, and the obligation to preserve the rights of its citizens and their personal privacy on the other. The purpose of this chapter is to evaluate public attitudes toward government organizations, particularly law enforcement organizations, as they relate to the protection of personal privacy.

1. Findings

Do Government Organizations Ask For Too Much Personal Information?

Despite all of the news coverage of alleged violations of personal privacy committed by the FBI and other law enforcement agencies in the past decade, the public seems to be more concerned about the Internal Revenue Service (38%) asking for too much personal information than it is about either the FBI (33%) or the CIA (34%). Among law enforcement agencies, the public is least concerned about local police asking for too much personal information (23%). Among all government institutions, the public is least concerned about the Social Security Administration (21%) and Congressional committees (22%).

Among the leadership groups, the government organizations which receive the most criticism are Congressional committees. Large pluralities, or majorities, of every leadership group except the Congressional respondents and executives in the computer industry feel that Congressional committees ask for too much personal information. The most critical groups are federal regulators (60%), executives in the insurance industry (63%), and business employers (57%).

Table 8-1

Government Organizations Which Ask For Too Much Personal Information: Public and Leaders

Question

I am going to read you a list of organizations and individuals which sometimes collect or use information about us. For each of these I would like you to tell me whether you feel they limit their personal information about individuals to what is really necessary or whether they ask for too much personal information.

| | | | Leaders | | | | | | | | | |
| | | | Privacy Intensive Industries | | | | | Government Officials | | | | |
(Number of respondents)	Total Public (1,511)	Business Employers (200)	Credit (32)	Credit Card (40)	Banks (36)	Insurance (36)	Computer (36)	State Insurance Commissioners (33)	Congress (77)	Law Enforcement Officials (42)	Regulatory Officials (53)	Doctors (33)
	%	%	%	%	%	%	%	%	%	%	%	%
Internal Revenue Service	38	27	25	23	11	25	25	42	31	21	26	33
The CIA	34	27	31	20	6	22	11	22	36	17	32	36
The FBI	33	29	19	25	11	25	28	38	53	21	47	45
Government welfare agencies	32	22	19	8	11	28	19	18	42	17	47	24
The Census Bureau	24	32	13	23	28	17	25	52	39	21	17	30
Local police	23	11	9	13	6	6	11	6	35	21	36	12
Congressional committees	22	57	47	45	50	63	36	45	22	37	60	42
Social Security Administration	21	10	3	3	–	11	6	15	17	7	13	18

(Note: See Table 2-8 for the percentages who believe these organizations limit their demands for information to what is necessary.)

2. Findings

The FBI: The Balance Between Protecting Individual Rights and Protecting Society

The government agency which has had the most public notoriety for the types of personal information it has gathered on the people, and the means it has used to gather it, has been the FBI. Indeed, in the last few years the FBI, more than any other government agency, has been accused of violating the privacy of numerous citizens. Nevertheless, when asked, only 1 in 3 Americans (34%) feel that the FBI is not doing enough to protect the rights of individuals. While 1 in 5 (21%) feel, on the contrary, that the FBI is not doing enough to protect society, and 26% feel that the FBI has got the balance between the rights of the individual and the protection of society about right.

Not surprisingly the attitudes of law enforcement officials on the one hand, and the congress and regulatory officials on the other are strikingly different.

Table 8-2

Whether FBI has Balanced Individual Rights and Protection of Society: Public and Leaders

Question

*The FBI has to try and balance its respect for the individual's constitutional rights against the need to conduct surveillance to protect society. Would you say that it has got the balance about right, **or** that it is not doing enough to protect individuals' constitutional rights, **or** that it is not doing enough to protect society?*

	(Number Of Respondents)	Got Balance About Right	Not Doing Enough To Protect Society	Not Doing Enough To Protect Individuals' Rights	Not Sure
Total Public	**(1,503)**	**26%**	**21%**	**34%**	**19%**
Age					
18–29	(420)	23%	18%	42%	17%
30–49	(560)	26%	22%	35%	17%
50 and over	(518)	30%	22%	27%	21%
Education					
8th grade	(135)	22%	21%	24%	33%
High school	(748)	27%	22%	33%	19%
College	(610)	27%	20%	39%	15%
Race					
White	(1,311)	28%	21%	34%	17%
Black	(110)	18%	16%	42%	23%
Political Philosophy					
Conservative	(484)	32%	25%	27%	16%
Middle-of-the-road	(567)	25%	21%	35%	19%
Liberal	(260)	20%	14%	50%	15%
Leaders					
Government Officials					
Congress	(76)	50%	11%	34%	5%
Law enforcement officials	(41)	46%	39%	10%	5%
Regulatory officials	(52)	31%	4%	58%	8%

Privacy

---

3. Findings

Obtaining Evidence and Court Orders

One of the great legal debates of the past decade has centered on the conditions under which a law enforcement agency should require a court order when it is obtaining information in a covert manner about the members of an organization who have never been convicted of a crime. In this regard, the survey finds that overwhelming majorities of both the public and leaders feel that a law enforcement agency **should not be able** *to open the mail, tap the telephones, or look at the bank records of individuals without a court order.*

By a 55–42% majority the public believes that law enforcement agencies should be able to keep the movements of suspected individuals under surveillance without a court order, while a majority of Congressional respondents (53%) and federal regulatory officials (55%) believe they should **not** *be able to do this without a court order. The overwhelming majority of law enforcement officials (90%) believe that they should be able to keep the movements of these individuals under surveillance without a court order.*

The public is rather divided (48–45%) as to whether a law enforcement agency should be allowed to place an undercover agent into these types of organizations without obtaining a court order. A majority of law enforcement officials (85%) believes that a court should not be required to do this, while majorities of Congressional respondents (61%) and regulatory officials (62%) feel that a court order should be required.

Table 8-3

Should Police Be Allowed to Take Certain Steps Without a Court Order: Public and Leaders

Question

When the police believe that members of an organization never convicted of a crime might engage in illegal acts in the future, do you think they should or should not be able to take the following steps **without obtaining a court order?**

| | | Leaders | | |
| | | Government Officials | | |
	Total Public (1,513)	Congress (77)	Law Enforcement Officials (42)	Regulatory Officials (53)
Keeping their movements under surveillance				
Should be able	55%	40%	90%	42%
Should not be able	42%	53%	10%	55%
Not sure	3%	6%	–	4%
Putting undercover agents into the organization				
Should be able	48%	34%	86%	30%
Should not be able	45%	61%	12%	62%
Not sure	6%	5%	2%	8%
Looking into their bank records				
Should be able	15%	1%	21%	8%
Should not be able	81%	97%	76%	89%
Not sure	4%	1%	2%	4%
Tapping their telephone				
Should be able	11%	3%	5%	–
Should not be able	87%	96%	93%	98%
Not sure	3%	1%	2%	2%
Opening their mail				
Should be able	7%	1%	2%	–
Should not be able	92%	99%	95%	98%
Not sure	2%	–	2%	2%

Privacy

4. Findings

Should The Police Have The Right To Demand Identification

*Majorities of the public (72%), those in Congress (84%), and federal regulatory officials (81%) feel that the police should **not** have the right to stop anyone on the street and demand to see some identification if the person is not doing anything illegal. The law enforcement officers are divided 45–43% on this question.*

Table 8-4

Should Police Have Right To Demand Identification Even If The Person Is Not Doing Anything Illegal: Public And Leaders

Question

Do you think the police should have the right to stop anyone on the street and demand to see some identification even if the person is not doing anything illegal, or shouldn't they have this right?

	(Number Of Respondents)	Should Have	Should Not Have	Not Sure
Total Public	**(1,511)**	**24%**	**72%**	**4%**
Leaders				
Government Officials				
Congress	*(77)*	*13%*	*84%*	*3%*
Law enforcement officials	*(42)*	*43%*	*45%*	*12%*
Regulatory officials	*(52)*	*13%*	*81%*	*6%*

5. Findings

The Use Of Lie Detectors In Government

Most of the public and most law enforcement officials do not feel the use of lie detectors under certain conditions is necessarily an intrusive manner of collecting information. Majorities of the public (58%) and law enforcement officers (67%) believe it is all right to use a lie detector to determine who has leaked confidential information from a government agency. A majority of Congressional respondents (65%) and regulatory officials (72%) disagree and do not think that it is all right to use a lie detector under these conditions.

Table 8-5

Whether Government Agency Should Use Lie Detector Test To Learn Source Of Information Leak: Public And Leaders

Question

If someone works in a government agency that uses classified information and there is a leak to the press, do you think it is or is not all right to make all those employees who handle the information take a lie detector test to learn who leaked the information?

	(Number Of Respondents)	Yes, It Is All Right	No, It Is Not All Right	It Depends (vol.)	Not Sure
Total Public	**(1,511)**	**58%**	**29%**	**10%**	**3%**
Leaders					
Congress	*(77)*	*27%*	*65%*	*6%*	*1%*
Law enforcement officials	*(42)*	*67%*	*24%*	*7%*	*2%*
Regulatory officials	*(53)*	*17%*	*72%*	*9%*	*2%*

Government Protection Of Confidential Personal Information

The government institutions which are most criticized by the public on the measure of confidentiality are government welfare agencies and the Internal Revenue Service. By 41% to 35% the public feels that government welfare agencies should be doing more to keep the personal information they have on individuals confidential. By 44% to 37% a plurality feels that the Internal Revenue Service is doing enough to keep personal information they have confidential. While a substantial 48% to 34% plurality believes that the local police are doing enough to protect personal privacy, small pluralities feel that the CIA and the FBI should be doing better.

Among the leadership groups, the greatest criticism is directed not at the Internal Revenue Service or government welfare agencies, but at Congressional committees. Majorities, or large minorities, of all the leadership groups feel that Congressional committees should be doing more to keep the personal information they have confidential. The most notable majority on this measure are the Congressional respondents. Fifty-three percent of Congressional respondents feel that the organizations they work for should be doing more to keep personal information confidential.

Table 8-6

Whether The Government Should Be Doing More To Maintain Confidentiality Of Personal Information: Public

Question

Now I'm going to read you the same list of organizations again. This time I would like you to tell me whether each organization is currently doing enough to keep the personal information they have on individuals confidential, or should they be doing more?

	Total Public		
(Number of respondents: 1,504)	Should Be Doing More	Doing Enough	Not Sure
Government welfare agencies	41%	35%	25%
Internal Revenue Service	37%	44%	19%
The FBI	35%	31%	34%
The CIA	34%	25%	41%
Local police	34%	48%	18%
Congressional committees	31%	27%	42%
Social Security Administration	27%	49%	24%
The Census Bureau	26%	52%	22%

Privacy

Table 8-7 **Whether The Government Should Be Doing More To Maintain Confidentiality of Personal Information: Leaders**

Question

Now I'm going to read you the same list of organizations again. This time I would like you to tell me whether each organization is currently doing enough to keep the personal information they have on individuals confidential, or should they be doing more?

		Leaders									
		Privacy Intensive Industry					Government Officials				
(Number of respondents)	Business Employers (200)	Credit (32)	Credit Card (40)	Banks (36)	Insur- ance (36)	Com- puter (36)	State Insurance Commis- sioners (32)	Congress (77)	Law Enforce- ment Offi- cials (42)	Regu- latory Offi- cials (52)	Doctors (33)
Government welfare agencies	36%	31%	20%	3%	33%	37%	38%	40%	19%	49%	41%
Internal Revenue Service	43%	38%	33%	22%	33%	39%	44%	42%	21%	44%	52%
The FBI	38%	31%	23%	6%	28%	34%	35%	42%	17%	48%	38%
The CIA	32%	19%	20%	11%	23%	31%	23%	32%	15%	35%	34%
Local police	24%	19%	20%	11%	25%	29%	35%	52%	21%	54%	26%
Congressional committees	59%	50%	45%	61%	65%	51%	53%	53%	44%	65%	50%
Social Security Administration	18%	6%	10%	6%	14%	20%	25%	25%	7%	27%	28%
The Census Bureau	26%	19%	23%	17%	8%	20%	31%	22%	19%	17%	25%

(Note: See Table 2-9 for the percentages who believe these organizations are doing enough to protect the confidentiality of personal information.)

---

7. Findings

Privacy and the Census Bureau

*Despite the fact that the Census Bureau is the least criticized government organization (26% of the public feel that it should be doing more to keep personal information confidential), there is a great deal of doubt among both the public and leaders that the Census Bureau is **not** sharing its information with other government agencies. Forty-five percent of the public is either "not too confident" or "not at all confident" that the Census Bureau protects the privacy of personal information about individuals and does not share it with other government agencies. Several of the leadership groups are even less confident than the public—72% of doctors, 59% of state insurance commissioners, 55% of business employers, 53% of credit card company executives, and 52% of executives in the credit business are either "not too confident" or "not at all confident" that the Census Bureau is protecting the privacy of personal information about individuals.*

Observation

As there has never been a case on the public record of the Census Bureau having shared with another government organization the personal information it gathered on an individual, the findings suggest that the credibility of the Census Bureau has suffered from the current mistrust of government.

Chapter 9

The Privacy
Intensive Industries:

Computers

Privacy

Objectives	*In a very real sense, computers are at the heart of the concerns over the loss and potential loss of privacy of personal data. The purpose of this chapter is to explore attitudes toward computers and the uses made of them by government and business.*

1. Findings	**Do Americans Believe Computers Threaten Privacy?**

A slim majority of Americans (54 to 31%) consider the present uses of computers as an actual threat to personal privacy in this country. The percentage of people who share this perception has risen 17 points since 1976, when only 37% felt that computers were a threat to personal privacy.

*Among the leadership groups, a majority of business employers (54%) state insurance commissioners (61%), Congressional respondents (75%), regulatory officials (75%), and doctors (70%) also feel that computers are a threat. Most importantly, 53% of those in the computer industry itself also believe that computers are a threat to personal privacy. Majorities of executives in the remaining privacy intensive industries and a plurality of law enforcement officials believe that computers are **not** a threat to personal privacy.*

Table 9-1	**Do Computers Threaten Privacy: Public and Leaders**
Question	*And now some questions on **computers**. Do you feel that the present uses of computers are an actual threat to personal privacy in the country, or not?*

	(Number Of Respondents)	Present Uses Are A Threat	Not A Threat	Not Sure
Total Public				
1978				
December	(1,509)	54%	31%	14%
January	(1,458)	54%	33%	13%
1977	(1,522)	41%	44%	15%
1976	(1,532)	37%	51%	12%
1974	(1,495)	38%	41%	21%
Age				
18–29	(424)	53%	35%	12%
30–49	(561)	55%	33%	12%
50 and over	(519)	55%	26%	18%
Education				
8th grade	(136)	50%	17%	33%
High school	(750)	56%	30%	14%
College	(613)	54%	36%	10%
Income				
Under $7,000	(280)	54%	22%	24%
$7,000–$14,999	(420)	55%	32%	13%
$15,000–$24,999	(490)	57%	34%	10%
$25,000 and over	(231)	53%	36%	11%
Leaders				
Business employers	(199)	54%	42%	4%
Privacy Intensive Industry				
Credit	(32)	34%	63%	3%
Credit card	(40)	25%	75%	–
Banks	(36)	22%	78%	–
Insurance	(36)	33%	64%	3%
Computer	(36)	53%	44%	3%
Government Officials				
State insurance commissioners	(33)	61%	33%	6%
Congress	(77)	75%	23%	1%
Law enforcement officials	(42)	48%	45%	7%
Regulatory officials	(53)	75%	25%	–
Doctors	(33)	70%	24%	6%

2. Findings

Some General Views of Computers

The public acknowledges by a 60–28% majority that computers have improved the quality of life in our society, and by a 64–23% majority it agrees that because computers can make use of more personal details about people, companies can provide customers with more individualized service.

Nevertheless, the American people are quite clear about their fears of computers as threats to personal privacy:

- By an 80–10% majority, they agree that computers have made it easier for someone to improperly obtain confidential personal information about individuals;
- By a 52–27% majority, they disagree that the privacy of personal information in computers is adequately safeguarded.

It is not surprising, then, that 63% of the public agrees with the statement that "if privacy is to be preserved, the use of computers must be sharply restricted in the future."

The leaders are at odds with the public on the necessity of restricting the future uses of computers, and majorities or pluralities of every group, except doctors, disagree with the statement that "if privacy is to be preserved, the use of computers must be sharply restricted in the future."

The leaders in the credit and insurance industries are at odds with the public and the remaining groups of leaders as to whether there are adequate safeguards for the protection of personal information in computers.

Observation

Clearly, public opinion regarding the use of computers should be of concern to the entire business community and the government and not just to the computer industry. The message is loud and clear—if the institutions of this society expect to be able to continue making widespread use of computers, the public must be convinced that the personal information stored in computers is adequately protected from improper use. The fact that a majority (53%) of respondents in the computer industry do not believe there are currently adequate safeguards governing the use of computers suggests much work needs to be done in this area.

Privacy

Table 9-2	**Agreement With Statements About Computers: Public and Leaders**
Question	*I'd like to read you some statements that people have made about computers. would like you to tell me whether you agree or disagree with each statement.*

		Leaders										
		Privacy Intensive Industries					Government Officials					
(Number of respondents)	Total Public (1,510)	Business Employers (200)	Credit (32)	Credit Card (40)	Banks (36)	Insur- ance (36)	Com- puter (36)	State Insurance Commis- sioners (33)	Congress (77)	Law Enforce- ment Offi- cials (42)	Regu- latory Offi- cials (53)	Doctors (33)
	%	%	%	%	%	%	%	%	%	%	%	%
Computers have made it much easier for someone to obtain confidential personal information about individuals improperly												
Agree	80	78	66	53	36	72	67	79	88	64	92	94
Disagree	10	21	31	48	58	28	33	15	9	26	4	6
Not sure	10	1	3	–	6	–	–	6	3	10	4	–
Because computers can make use of more personal details about people, companies can provide customers with more individualized service than before												
Agree	64	79	81	90	81	78	86	67	64	81	57	61
Disagree	23	16	16	10	11	19	14	33	31	17	36	33
Not sure	13	6	3	–	8	3	–	–	5	2	8	6
If privacy is to be preserved, the use of computers must be sharply restricted in the future												
Agree	63	31	19	13	8	25	8	36	35	31	42	55
Disagree	20	66	81	85	86	69	89	55	57	60	50	42
Not sure	16	4	–	3	6	6	3	9	8	10	8	3
Computers have improved the quality of life in our society												
Agree	60	88	94	98	89	94	97	67	86	83	74	73
Disagree	28	10	6	3	11	6	3	24	13	14	19	18
Not sure	13	2	–	–	–	–	–	9	1	2	8	9
In general, the privacy of personal information in computers is adequately safeguarded												
Agree	27	43	59	80	78	61	42	16	22	43	9	18
Disagree	52	48	34	15	17	28	53	69	65	48	75	76
Not sure	21	9	6	5	6	11	6	16	13	10	15	6

3. Findings

Reactions to Potential Uses of Computers

In order to obtain an additional perspective of public concern about the threats to personal privacy posed by computers, respondents were read a list of five different circumstances in which computers could be used, and were asked whether they considered each use justified or not. The findings show that the American people are not opposed to the use of computers in every situation:

- *By 87 to 9%, they believe it is justifiable to use computers to check welfare rolls against employment records to identify people claiming benefits to which they are not entitled;*
- *By a solid majority of 68 to 23%, they believe it is acceptable for the Internal Revenue Service to use computers to check tax returns against credit records;*
- *Finally, a slight majority of 53 to 40% believes that the insurance industry is justified in maintaining a central file containing the details of anyone who is* **suspected** *of making a fraudulent claim on any insurance policy.*

However, by a 68 to 24% majority the public does not feel it is justifiable to use computers to maintain a central file containing the names of all individuals who have been treated for mental health problems for use by employers. A somewhat smaller majority (51%) also feels it is not justifiable for state agencies to use computers to maintain a central file containing a record of names of individuals who have been given a prescription for a dangerous or addictive drug.

Overwhelming majorities of all leadership groups feel that the use of a computer to check welfare rolls against employment records is warranted. However, majorities of all leadership groups also agree with the public that the use of computers to maintain a central file containing the names of individuals who have been given a prescription for a dangerous or addictive drug is not justifiable. The leaders also agree that computers should not be used to maintain a central file of names of all who have been treated for mental health problems for use by employers.

A majority of all leadership groups, except those executives in the insurance industry, believe that it is **not** *justifiable for the insurance industry to use computers to keep central files containing the details of anyone who is* **suspected** *of making a fraudulent claim on any insurance policy.*

Majorities or pluralities of all leadership groups, except executives in the credit card industry, those in Congress, and doctors, feel that it is justifiable for the Internal Revenue Service to use computers to check tax returns against credit cards.

The public's differing responses to differing issues reveals its inherent pragmatism.

Privacy

Table 9-3	Whether Various Uses of Computers are Justified: Public and Leaders
Question	I am going to read to you a number of different ways that computers could be used today. I would like you to tell me whether each type of use is justified or not.

		Leaders										
		Privacy Intensive Industries					Government Officials				
	Total Public	Business Employers	Credit	Credit Card	Banks	Insur- ance	Com- puter	State Insurance Commis- sioners	Congress	Law Enforce- ment Offi- cials	Regu- latory Offi- cials	Doctors
(Number of respondents)	(1,510)	(200)	(32)	(40)	(36)	(36)	(36)	(35)	(77)	(42)	(52)	(33)
	%	%	%	%	%	%	%	%	%	%	%	%
Government agencies checking welfare rolls against employment records to identify people claiming benefits they are not entitled to												
Justified	87	96	94	98	100	92	92	91	91	98	85	97
Not justified	9	4	6	3	–	6	8	9	6	2	12	3
Not sure	4	1	–	–	–	3	–	–	3	–	4	–
Internal Revenue Service using computers to check tax returns against credit card records												
Justified	68	54	59	43	72	58	61	58	45	76	50	45
Not justified	23	45	38	55	25	36	39	39	52	21	46	48
Not sure	9	2	3	3	3	6	–	3	3	2	4	6
*The insurance industry maintaining a central file containing details of anyone who is **suspected** of making a fraudulent claim on any insurance policy*												
Justified	53	26	6	28	14	58	25	45	17	38	12	18
Not justified	40	73	88	73	81	39	75	55	83	62	87	82
Not sure	7	2	6	–	6	3	–	–	–	–	2	–
State agencies maintaining a central file containing a record of the names of individuals who have been given a prescription for a dangerous or addictive drug												
Justified	40	22	9	15	14	22	36	18	14	36	25	21
Not justified	51	74	91	80	86	69	61	79	84	62	69	79
Not sure	8	5	–	5	–	8	3	3	1	2	6	–
Maintaining a central file containing the names of all individuals who have been treated for mental health problems for use by employers												
Justified	24	6	6	8	3	14	11	6	5	19	4	–
Not justified	68	93	91	93	92	86	83	94	95	76	94	100
Not sure	8	2	3	–	6	–	6	–	–	5	2	–

Chapter 10

Privacy
In The Future

Privacy

This chapter is concerned with what Americans feel their privacy situation will be like in the future.

---

1. Findings

How Close Are We to a "Big Brother" Society

*One in three Americans (34%) believes that this society is very close to—or already like—the type of society described by George Orwell in his book **1984**, a society in which "virtually all personal privacy had been lost and the government knew almost everything that everyone was doing." Furthermore, 73% feel that we are somewhat close or closer.*

*The leadership groups (with the exception of doctors) are much less likely to feel that this society is close to approximating the society George Orwell describes in **1984**. The greatest concern in this regard is shown by the senior executives of credit companies, of whom 25% feel that we are already at or very close to being a society in which the government knows almost everything about everyone. At 39% doctors are slightly more likely than the public to believe we are close to the society described in **1984**.*

Table 10-1

How Close Are We to a "Big Brother" Society: Public and Leaders

Question

*In a book, **1984**, by George Orwell, virtually all personal privacy had been lost and the government—called "Big Brother"—knew almost everything that everyone was doing. Whether or not you have read the book, how close do you think we are to that kind of society—are we there already, very close, somewhat close, or not close at all?*

	(Number Of Respondents)	We Are There Already	Very Close	Some-what Close	Not At All Close	Not Sure
Total Public	**(1,510)**	**8%**	**26%**	**39%**	**19%**	**8%**
Leaders						
Business employers	(200)	2%	21%	54%	24%	–
Privacy Intensive Industry						
Credit	(32)	3%	22%	53%	22%	–
Credit card	(40)	3%	13%	40%	45%	–
Banks	(36)	–	8%	50%	39%	3%
Insurance	(36)	–	11%	53%	36%	–
Computer	(36)	–	14%	50%	36%	–
Government Officials						
State insurance commissioners	(33)	9%	18%	45%	27%	–
Congress	(77)	1%	9%	52%	38%	–
Law enforcement officials	(42)	–	10%	40%	48%	2%
Regulatory officials	(52)	2%	17%	54%	27%	–
Doctors	(33)	6%	33%	39%	21%	–

| 2. Findings | **Ability of Individuals to Maintain Their Privacy in Relation to the Government 10 Years From Now** |

Further evidence of the public's wariness of government noted in earlier chapters is shown by the findings that—51% to 38%—the public believes we will have lost much of our ability to keep important aspects of our life from the government in 10 years time.

Again with the exception of doctors, leaders are less cynical than the public in this regard.

| Table 10-2 | **Ability to Maintain Privacy From Government Ten Years From Now: Public and Leaders** |

| Question | *When you think about what life in the U.S. will be like 10 years from now, do you believe we will have lost much of our ability to keep important aspects of our lives private from the government, or do you believe we will still be able to keep our privacy free from unreasonable invasions by government?* |

	(Number Of Respondents)	*Will Have Lost Much*	*Will Still Be Able To Keep Privacy*	*Not Sure*
Total Public	**(1,513)**	**51%**	**38%**	**11%**
Leaders				
Business employers	(200)	42%	55%	4%
Privacy Intensive Industry				
Credit	(32)	41%	56%	3%
Credit card	(40)	23%	75%	3%
Banks	(35)	20%	80%	–
Insurance	(36)	19%	75%	6%
Computer	(36)	47%	53%	–
Government Officials				
State insurance commissioners	(32)	38%	63%	–
Congress	(77)	32%	61%	6%
Law enforcement officials	(41)	37%	63%	–
Regulatory officials	(52)	42%	54%	4%
Doctors	(33)	64%	30%	6%

| 3. Findings | **Whether Laws Can Help Protect Privacy** |

A majority (67%) of the public feels that new laws and organizational policies "could go a long way to help preserve our privacy."

Majorities of business employers (58%), executives in the insurance (64%) and computer industries (72%), state insurance commissioners (81%), Congressional respondents (82%), regulatory officials (87%), and doctors (79%) also feel that laws and policies could help. However, executives in credit institutions (50%), the credit card industry (50%), and banking (43%) are much less enthusiastic, as are law enforcement officials (48%).

Privacy

Observation	Throughout the study it has been apparent that the public is concerned about the potential for loss of personal privacy.	It is quite clear that the public is asking—perhaps demanding—that government and business organizations take effective measures to help prevent future loss of personal privacy.
	This fear is confirmed here, as we note that the public believes it will have lost much of its privacy in relation to the government, and the feeling that new laws could help stem that loss of privacy.	

Table 10-3   **Can Laws Help Preserve Privacy: Public and Leaders**

Question   *Do you think that new laws and organizational policies could go a long way to help preserve our privacy, or do you think there is nothing much that can be done to keep our privacy from being eroded?*

	(Number Of Respondents)	Laws And Policies Could Help	Nothing Much That Can Be Done	Laws Not Needed (vol.)	Not Sure
Total Public	**(1,510)**	**67%**	**23%**	**–**	**10%**
Leaders					
Business employers	(197)	58%	16%	21%	5%
Privacy Intensive Industry					
Credit	(32)	50%	9%	38%	3%
Credit card	(40)	50%	8%	43%	–
Banks	(35)	43%	11%	43%	3%
Insurance	(33)	64%	9%	21%	6%
Computer	(36)	72%	8%	8%	11%
Government Officials					
State insurance commissioners	(32)	81%	9%	9%	–
Congress	(77)	82%	6%	10%	1%
Law enforcement officials	(42)	48%	10%	31%	12%
Regulatory officials	(53)	87%	6%	8%	–
Doctors	(33)	79%	3%	15%	3%

| 4. Findings | **The Need for a National Privacy Protection Agency** |

There is no widespread support among either the public or the leaders for a National Privacy Protection Agency. By a 46–37% plurality the public opposes the creation of such an agency. Large majorities of all the leadership groups also oppose the creation of such an agency.

| **Observation** | *The public wants laws and business policies to protect their future privacy; they do not believe that a new government agency can do the job.* |

| **Table 10-4** | **Should There be a National Privacy Protection Agency: Public and Leaders** |

| **Question** | *Some people believe that a new National Privacy Protection Agency should be set up if the privacy of individual citizens is to be protected in this country. Other people believe that such a national agency would merely lead to more intrusions into our personal privacy. Would you favor or oppose the creation of a National Privacy Protection Agency?* |

	(Number Of Respondents)	Favor	Oppose	Not Sure
Total Public	**(1,502)**	**37%**	**46%**	**17%**
Leaders				
Business employers	(200)	6%	93%	2%
Privacy Intensive Industry				
Credit	(32)	6%	94%	–
Credit card	(39)	3%	97%	–
Banks	(36)	3%	97%	–
Insurance	(36)	3%	97%	–
Computer	(36)	17%	72%	11%
Government Officials				
State insurance commissioners	(33)	–	97%	3%
Congress	(76)	7%	88%	5%
Law enforcement officials	(42)	10%	88%	2%
Regulatory officials	(53)	23%	77%	–
Doctors	(33)	18%	76%	6%

Privacy

5. Findings

Whether an Independent Body Set Up to Handle Privacy Complaints Would be Desirable

The public and the leaders are in sharp disagreement over the preferability of an independent body or agency to handle complaints about violations of personal privacy by an organization. Sixty-two percent of the public feel that such an organization is "very important" while majorities of every leadership group—except those in the computer industry, regulatory officials, and doctors—feels that such an agency is "not at all important."

Observation

On this issue the very wide gap between the public and the leadership suggests that the establishment is out of touch.

Table 10-5

Importance of Agency to Handle Privacy Violation Complaints: Public and Leaders

Question

Thinking of organizations such as banks, insurance companies, private employers, and credit card companies, how important is it that there should be an independent body or agency to handle complaints about violations of personal privacy by an organization?

	(Number Of Respondents)	Very Important	Somewhat Important	Not Important At All	Not Sure
Total Public	**(1,510)**	**62%**	**19%**	**11%**	**7%**
Leaders					
Business employers	(200)	18%	18%	59%	5%
Privacy Intensive Industry					
Credit	(32)	22%	19%	59%	–
Credit card	(40)	8%	10%	80%	3%
Banks	(36)	14%	14%	72%	–
Insurance	(36)	17%	14%	64%	6%
Computer	(36)	28%	19%	36%	17%
Government Officials					
State insurance commissioners	(33)	9%	18%	67%	6%
Congress	(77)	18%	14%	64%	4%
Law enforcement officials	(42)	26%	14%	60%	–
Regulatory officials	(53)	32%	21%	42%	6%
Doctors	(33)	39%	27%	33%	–

6. Findings

Importance of Collecting Only Essential Information and of Communicating Why it is Important to Collect That Information

In order to determine what types of information are considered appropriate to collect, respondents were asked to indicate how important it is for an organization to collect only the information on individuals that is essential to make a proper decision. The table below clearly shows that large majorities of the public (84%) and of all of the leadership groups feel that it is "very important" to ask only for the information essential to making a decision.

Table 10-6

Importance of Collecting Only Essential Personal Information: Public and Leaders

Question

Thinking of organizations such as banks, insurance companies, private employers, and credit card companies, how important is it that they collect only the personal information on individuals which is essential to make a proper decision?

	(Number Of Respondents)	Very Important	Somewhat Important	Not Important At All	Not Sure
Total Public	**(1,510)**	**84%**	**12%**	**2%**	**2%**
Leaders					
Business employers	(200)	85%	13%	2%	1%
Privacy Intensive Industry					
Credit	(32)	91%	9%	–	–
Credit card	(40)	79%	13%	8%	–
Banks	(36)	83%	17%	–	–
Insurance	(36)	86%	14%	–	–
Computer	(36)	81%	19%	–	–
Government Officials					
State insurance commissioners	(33)	91%	9%	–	–
Congress	(77)	88%	12%	–	–
Law enforcement officials	(42)	90%	7%	–	2%
Regulatory officials	(53)	94%	6%	–	–
Doctors	(33)	91%	9%	–	–

In order for an organization to communicate more effectively with the individuals on whom it is gathering information, two procedures are considered important. Fully 88% of the public feels that when an organization collects information on individuals it should tell them just how that information will be used. Majorities of all leaders except those in the credit industry share this feeling with the public.

Privacy

Table 10-7		Importance of Telling How Information Will be Used: Public and Leaders				
Question		*Thinking of organizations such as banks, private employers, and credit card companies, how important is it that they tell individuals when information is collected on them just how that information will be used?*				

	(Number Of Respondents)	Very Important	Somewhat Important	Not Important At All	Not Sure
Total Public	**(1,510)**	**88%**	**9%**	**2%**	**2%**
Leaders					
Business employers	(200)	70%	24%	7%	–
Privacy Intensive Industry					
Credit	(32)	47%	41%	13%	–
Credit card	(40)	43%	30%	28%	–
Banks	(36)	47%	31%	22%	–
Insurance	(36)	61%	25%	14%	–
Computer	(36)	67%	31%	3%	–
Government Officials					
State insurance commissioners	(33)	76%	15%	9%	–
Congress	(77)	82%	16%	3%	–
Law enforcement officials	(42)	74%	21%	5%	–
Regulatory officials	(53)	91%	4%	4%	2%
Doctors	(33)	76%	21%	3%	–

And 74% of the public believe that it is important that organizations should provide a separate written explanation of why each piece of information is needed for anyone who asks for it. Majorities of government officials, doctors, and executives in the insurance and computer industries concur.

Table 10-8	**Importance of Explaining in Writing Why Information is Needed: Public and Leaders**			
Question	When someone fills out an application for credit, insurance, employment, or a government benefit there are many questions which are asked for reasons which may not be obvious. One suggestion is that the organization make available a separate written explanation of why each piece of information is needed to anyone who asks for it. Do you think this is important or not really necessary?			
	(Number Of Respondents)	*Important*	*Not Really Necessary*	*Sure*
Total Public	**(1,512)**	**74%**	**23%**	**3%**
Leaders				
Business employers	*(200)*	*48%*	*53%*	*–*
Privacy Intensive Industry				
Credit	*(32)*	*38%*	*63%*	*–*
Credit card	*(40)*	*23%*	*78%*	*–*
Banks	*(34)*	*26%*	*74%*	*–*
Insurance	*(36)*	*53%*	*47%*	*–*
Computer	*(36)*	*61%*	*36%*	*3%*
Government officials				
State insurance commissioners	*(32)*	*59%*	*41%*	*–*
Congress	*(76)*	*72%*	*26%*	*1%*
Law enforcement officials	*(42)*	*71%*	*29%*	*–*
Regulatory officials	*(53)*	*77%*	*23%*	*–*
Doctors	*(33)*	*85%*	*15%*	*–*

7. Findings

Whether Organizations Should Get Permission From Individuals Before Releasing Their Personal Information

The survey finds that majorities of the public (91%) and of all of the leadership groups feel that an organization should obtain an individual's agreement before information from his file is given out to other organizations for purposes other than what it was collected for.

Privacy

Table 10-9	**Importance of Obtaining Permission to Release Information From File: Public and Leaders**				
Question	*Thinking of organizations such as banks, insurance companies, private employers, and credit card companies, how important is it that they obtain an individual's agreement before information from his file is given out to other organizations for purposes other than what it was collected for?*				
	(Number Of Respondents)	*Very Important*	*Somewhat Important*	*Not Important At All*	*Not Sure*
Total Public	**(1,510)**	**91%**	**5%**	**2%**	**2%**
Leaders					
Business employers	*(200)*	*93%*	*6%*	*1%*	*1%*
Privacy Intensive Industry					
Credit	*(32)*	*81%*	*9%*	*9%*	*–*
Credit card	*(40)*	*75%*	*15%*	*10%*	*–*
Banks	*(36)*	*72%*	*19%*	*8%*	*–*
Insurance	*(36)*	*83%*	*11%*	*6%*	*–*
Computer	*(36)*	*94%*	*6%*	*–*	*–*
Government Officials					
State insurance commissioners	*(33)*	*100%*	*–*	*–*	*–*
Congress	*(77)*	*94%*	*5%*	*–*	*1%*
Law enforcement officials	*(42)*	*88%*	*12%*	*–*	*–*
Regulatory officials	*(53)*	*96%*	*4%*	*–*	*–*
Doctors	*(33)*	*100%*	*–*	*–*	*–*

8. Findings	**Should Individuals be Able to See and Verify the Information in the Files**
	A large majority (85%) of the public feels it is "very important" that organizations give individuals a chance to see and verify what is in their own personal record, including what third parties have said. They are joined in this feeling by all of the leadership groups except those in the credit card and insurance industries. However, even among credit card and insurance executives, no more than 20% think that such access is not important at all.
Observation	*The public could not be more adamant in what should be done to protect their privacy. The public wants to play an active role with government and business in terms of reviewing their files and giving permission before such information is released. And, they want business and government to justify to them why information is to be collected, what it is and how it will be used.*

Table 10-10   **Importance of Verifying Information in Personal Record: Public and Leaders**

Question   *Thinking of organizations such as banks, insurance companies, private employers, and credit card companies, how important is it that they give individuals a chance to see and verify what is in their personal record including what third parties have said?*

	(Number Of Respondents)	Very Important	Somewhat Important	Not Important At All	Not Sure
Total Public	**(1,510)**	**85%**	**10%**	**3%**	**2%**
Leaders					
Business employers	(200)	61%	23%	14%	4%
Privacy Intensive Industry					
Credit	(32)	78%	3%	13%	6%
Credit card	(40)	45%	28%	20%	8%
Banks	(36)	58%	19%	22%	–
Insurance	(36)	50%	33%	14%	3%
Computer	(36)	72%	17%	8%	3%
Government Officials					
State insurance commissioners	(33)	73%	21%	6%	–
Congress	(77)	59%	26%	12%	3%
Law enforcement officials	(42)	74%	14%	7%	5%
Regulatory officials	(53)	79%	9%	9%	2%
Doctors	(33)	73%	21%	6%	–

---

9. Findings   **Who Should Have the Responsibility for Protecting Individuals Privacy**

The American people appear somewhat ambivalent in their feelings about who should be responsible for protecting their personal privacy. On the one hand, there is some evidence that they do not trust the business community, either as employers or as providers of services, to protect their personal privacy:

- *By a 65–25% majority the public thinks that a law should be passed specifying employees' rights of access to their personnel file rather than leaving decisions regarding such rights to employers (Table 3-12).*

- *By a 65–27% majority the public believes that the types of information that an insurance company is allowed to gather on an individual should be determined by law and not by the insurance companies (Table 5-6).*

On the other hand, there is no consensus among the public as to who should have the major responsibility for protecting the privacy of individuals. Thirty percent mention the courts, 26% the Congress, and 24% state government. Only 14% mention the President, and 12% employers. The leaders are most likely to mention the courts, with majorities of all leadership groups feeling that the courts should have the major responsibility for protecting the privacy of individuals. However, majorities of Congressional respondents and regulators also mention the Congress.

Privacy

Observation	Because of a lack of confidence in the capacity of the courts, government or the private sector to protect personal privacy, fully 49% of the public feels that the main responsibility for protecting the privacy of the individual should rest with the people themselves.

Table 10-11   **Where Responsibility for Protecting Privacy Should Lie: Public and Leaders**

Question	Which of these do you think should have a major responsibility for protecting the privacy of individuals in America?

	(Number Of Respondents)	The People Themselves	The Courts	The Congress	State Governments	The President	Employers	Not Sure
Total Public	**(1,504)**	**49%**	**30%**	**26%**	**24%**	**14%**	**12%**	**5%**
Leaders								
Business employers	(200)	72%	56%	38%	24%	19%	40%	1%
Privacy Intensive Industry								
Credit	(32)	53%	59%	41%	16%	9%	13%	3%
Credit card	(40)	63%	65%	33%	30%	15%	48%	–
Banks	(35)	83%	74%	23%	11%	11%	26%	–
Insurance	(36)	56%	53%	31%	19%	8%	42%	6%
Computer	(36)	69%	83%	53%	28%	25%	44%	–
Government Officials								
State insurance commissioners	(33)	70%	64%	33%	39%	15%	33%	–
Congress	(77)	60%	78%	61%	40%	34%	38%	–
Law enforcement officials	(40)	65%	58%	38%	28%	20%	30%	3%
Regulatory officials	(53)	68%	77%	77%	47%	47%	57%	–
Doctors	(33)	79%	67%	58%	42%	21%	45%	–

Chapter 11

Privacy

| Objectives | *The preceding chapter shows that the American people are concerned about their future privacy and want to play an active role with government and business in protecting it. This chapter deals with possible future legislation in privacy.* |

1. Findings

Leadership Views on the Need for Privacy Legislation

The leadership sample was asked to indicate which of four alternative approaches to future policies best described their view as to what is needed. The findings show that less than one in five among any of the leadership groups feel that no new policies are needed to define privacy rights in the private sector.

The business employers and executives in the credit and insurance industry are not inclined to believe that comprehensive and detailed legislation is needed. These groups are divided between giving the private sector a reasonable period of time to adopt new privacy protections voluntarily before legislation is enacted, and having the basic rights defined by law with specific ways of complying left up to individual companies.

The government officials are more reluctant to allow the private sector a reasonable period of time to adopt new privacy protections voluntarily. There is a greater preference among government officials for having the basic rights defined by law with specific ways of complying being left up to individual companies and having comprehensive and detailed legislation now.

Table 11-1

Views on Privacy Rights Legislation: Leaders

Question

Thinking about the private organizations that collect information about people, such as banks, insurance companies, and credit card firms, which one of these items best describes your view?

		Privacy Intensive Industry					Government Officials				
(Number of respondents)	Business Employers (199)	Credit (32)	Credit Card (40)	Banks (36)	Insur-ance (35)	Com-puter (36)	State Insurance Commis-sioners (33)	Congress (77)	Law Enforce-ment Offi-cials (41)	Regu-latory Offi-cials (53)	Doctors (33)
We don't need any new policies or laws to define privacy rights in the private sector	14%	19%	18%	14%	9%	6%	3%	9%	15%	2%	12%
The private sector should be allowed a reasonable period of time to adopt new privacy protections voluntarily; only if most firms fail to do so should legislation be enacted	38%	31%	43%	39%	49%	19%	18%	21%	15%	9%	6%
Basic rights should be defined by law, with specific ways of complying left up to the individual companies	27%	31%	35%	39%	34%	42%	36%	39%	27%	45%	36%
We need comprehensive and detailed legislation now to protect privacy in the major industries that use personal information extensively	21%	16%	5%	6%	3%	31%	39%	31%	32%	43%	42%
None (vol.)	1%	3%	–	–	6%	–	–	–	12%	–	–
Not sure	1%	–	–	3%	–	3%	3%	–	–	–	3%

| | | Privacy Intensive Industry | | | | |

2. Findings

Business' Views of Corporate Privacy Policy

In order to further refine the reading of the business community's attitudes toward privacy policy in the future, business executives were asked to indicate which of three courses of action best described their company's philosophy regarding job applicants and employees, and which best described their company's philosophy toward customers and clients.

In general, the business community, as represented by our sample, is divided about which is the best way to handle future privacy policy. Pluralities of executives in the credit and insurance industries say they want to adopt new privacy policies when a consensus is developed among employers in their industries about what is right to do. Executives in the banking (44%) and insurance industries (47%) especially favor this approach. Nevertheless, there are substantial minorities who want to "be a pioneer in adopting company policies" or "wait until laws are passed that define what is proper and improper to do." Business employers and computer executives are divided between waiting for a consensus to be developed and waiting until laws are passed that define what is proper and improper.

Table 11-2   **Company Policy Regarding Information About Applicants and Employees: Business Leaders**

Question   *In terms of your company adopting new privacy policies dealing with the information it collects and uses about people who are **job applicants and employees**, which one of these items best describes your company's philosophy?*

		Privacy Intensive Industry				
(Number of respondents)	Business Employers (200)	Credit (28)	Credit Card (38)	Banks (32)	Insurance (32)	Computer (35)
We want to be a pioneer in adopting company policies that provide new privacy protections	25%	32%	32%	25%	38%	11%
We want to adopt new privacy policies when a consensus is developed among employers of our type about what is right to do	33%	39%	34%	44%	47%	37%
We want to wait until laws are passed that define what is proper and improper to do, and we would then comply as good citizens	36%	25%	29%	25%	13%	40%
None (vol.)	5%	4%	--	3%	--	3%
Not sure	3%	--	5%	3%	3%	9%

Privacy

		Privacy Intensive Industry				
Table 11-3	**Company Policy Regarding Information About Customers and Clients:** **Business Leaders**					

Question — In terms of your company adopting new privacy policies dealing with the information it collects and uses about **customers and clients**, which one of these items best describes your company's philosophy?

	Business Employers (199)	Credit (28)	Credit Card (38)	Banks (32)	Insurance (33)	Computer (35)
(Number of respondents)						
We want to be a pioneer in adopting company policies that provide new privacy protections	14%	25%	26%	25%	30%	26%
We want to adopt new privacy policies when a consensus is developed in our industry about what is right to do	38%	43%	34%	31%	42%	37%
We want to wait until laws are passed that define what is proper and improper to do, and we would then comply as good citizens	38%	29%	29%	34%	27%	23%
None (vol.)	6%	4%	8%	3%	–	9%
Not sure	5%	–	3%	6%	–	6%

A similar division occurs with regard to new privacy policies as they relate to a company's clients and customers. In the credit (43%), credit card (34%), insurance (42%), and computer (37%) industries, pluralities favor adopting new privacy policies when a consensus is developed in their industry. Bankers are slightly more in favor of awaiting new laws that will define what is proper and improper to do (34%). Business employers in equal numbers want to await a consensus (38%) and await new laws (38%). Regardless, such substantial minorities of all leadership groups favor each option that the business community is best characterized as deeply divided over what the next step to take in privacy policy should be.

Table 11-4   **Areas in Which Legislation Should be Passed: Public and Leaders**

Question   *Although there are already some laws regulating what information private organizations can collect about individuals, Congress is currently considering passing additional privacy legislation. In which of the following areas do you think it is important that Congress pass legislation?*

| | | | Leaders | | | | | | | | | |
| | | | Privacy Intensive Industries | | | | | Government Officials | | | | |
Number of respondents)	Total Public (1,509)	Business Employers (200)	Credit (32)	Credit Card (40)	Banks (36)	Insurance (36)	Computer (36)	State Insurance Commissioners (33)	Congress (77)	Law Enforcement Officials (41)	Regulatory Officials (53)	Doctors (33)
	%	%	%	%	%	%	%	%	%	%	%	%
Medicine and health												
Important	65	38	22	30	19	42	53	42	57	29	72	55
Not important	29	58	69	68	78	50	44	58	38	66	19	39
Not sure	6	5	9	3	3	8	3	–	5	5	9	6
Insurance												
Important	65	38	19	20	8	39	53	36	57	34	72	61
Not important	28	59	75	80	92	58	44	64	39	59	21	33
Not sure	7	4	6	–	–	3	3	–	4	7	8	6
Employment												
Important	62	30	16	18	11	28	36	52	51	29	66	58
Not important	32	69	81	80	89	69	58	48	45	59	26	39
Not sure	6	1	3	3	–	3	6	–	4	12	8	3
Mailing Lists												
Important	61	60	56	33	28	39	56	67	56	61	60	73
Not important	33	38	44	68	72	53	44	33	43	34	30	24
Not sure	6	2	–	–	–	8	–	–	1	5	9	3
Credit cards												
Important	61	42	16	10	6	36	31	39	60	32	64	55
Not important	31	56	81	90	94	53	64	52	36	63	28	39
Not sure	8	3	3	–	–	11	6	9	4	5	8	6
Telephone company call records												
Important	51	32	19	28	17	33	47	45	57	27	58	55
Not important	40	64	72	73	83	50	50	45	36	66	23	39
Not sure	9	5	9	–	–	17	3	9	6	7	19	6
Public opinion polling												
Important	36	12	13	5	3	8	11	18	18	5	28	30
Not important	54	85	88	95	97	86	83	79	78	90	60	67
Not sure	10	3	–	–	–	6	6	3	4	5	11	3

Privacy

---

3. Findings

Areas Where Legislation Might Be Passed

When respondents are shown a list of areas where legislation is being considered for regulating the kind of information that an organization can collect, they make very few distinctions as to the importance of legislation in five of seven areas. At least 60% of the public believes that it is important to have laws regulating the type of information that organizations in the areas of credit cards (61%), medicine and health (65%), insurance (65%), employment (62%), and mailing lists (61%) can collect. Majorities of Congressional respondents and federal regulators feel that legislation is important in every area, except public opinion polling. The only area in which substantial numbers of executives in the privacy intensive areas (excluding the computer industry) agree legislation is important is that of mailing lists.

---

4. Findings

Importance of a Law Ensuring Confidentiality of State Files

The public feels quite strongly about the need for government agencies to protect the confidentiality of the personal information they collect. Fully 71% of the American people feel that it is "very important" that their states should have laws designed to ensure that the information in state files is kept confidential.

Table 11-5

Importance of Law Ensuring Confidentiality of State Files: Public

Question

How important is it to you that your state should have a law designed to ensure that the information in state files is kept confidential—very important, somewhat important, not too important, or not at all important?

	Total Public
(Number of respondents)	*(1,508)*
Very important	*71%*
Somewhat important	*18%*
Not too important	*5%*
Not at all important	*2%*
Not sure	*3%*

---

5. Findings

Central Controls and Identity Cards

Despite the great public concern with crime in this country, majorities of both the public and the leadership groups reject the suggestion that national identity cards be issued to help find suspected criminals and illegal aliens. They also reject the idea of a central government file containing personal information on all citizens. Opposition to both measures is greatest among Congressional respondents where 78% "oppose strongly" the need either for an identity card or a central file.

| | | Leaders | | |
| | | Government Officials | | |
(Number of respondents)	Total Public (1,512)	Congress (77)	Law Enforcement Officials (42)	Regulatory Officials (53)
Identity cards should be issued by the government to all Americans so that it would be easier to find suspected criminals and illegal aliens				
Favor strongly	23%	4%	31%	8%
Favor somewhat	14%	4%	5%	13%
Oppose somewhat	15%	14%	14%	6%
Oppose strongly	42%	78%	50%	74%
Not sure	5%	–	–	–
A government file should be kept of each citizen's tax record, military history, police record, and other records of his/her personal behavior, and used when some question of illegal conduct arises				
Favor strongly	13%	1%	17%	–
Favor somewhat	21%	8%	24%	13%
Oppose somewhat	21%	12%	21%	11%
Oppose strongly	40%	78%	38%	75%
Not sure	5%	1%	–	–

Table 11-6   **Whether Favor Specific Steps Toward Central Controls: Public and Leaders**

Question   *I will read you a few suggestions that people have made. For each, tell me if you would favor strongly, favor somewhat, oppose somewhat, or oppose strongly such a step being taken.*

Privacy

At the issue development level of this study, a hypothesis was formulated that the more alienated individuals feel they are from technology and the institutions of government and business, the more likely they are to be concerned about threats to their personal privacy.

In order to test this hypothesis, an alienation index was created by asking respondents to agree or disagree with the following four statements:

1. Technology has almost gotten out of control.

2. Government can generally be trusted to look after our interests

3. The way one votes has no effect on what the government does.

4. In general, business helps us more than it harms us.

"Agree" responses to items one and three or "disagree" responses to items two and four were considered alienated answers. Respondents were then placed into one of the four following categories:

1. Those respondents who gave alienated responses on at least three of the four items were categorized as highly alienated.

2. Those who gave alienated responses on two of the four items were considered to be moderately alienated.

3. Those who gave an alienated response to only one item were categorized as having a low level of alienation.

4. Those who did not give an alienated answer to any items were considered to be not alienated.

The survey finds that 21% of the total public can be categorized as being highly alienated from technology and the institutions of government and business. Another 28% are moderately alienated, and 34% fit into the low alienation category. Only 17% of the population can be considered to be not alienated.

Table P-1	**Public Alienation**	
		Total Public
High alienation		21%
Moderate alienation		28%
Low alienation		34%
Not alienated		17%

The most alienated groups in society are blacks, liberals, those who have only attended high school, skilled laborers, and those living in the West. The least alienated groups are those having professional occupations, residents of rural areas, Southerners, those with annual incomes of $25,000 and over, and white Protestants.

Table P-2   **Most/Least Alienated Groups: Public**

	Percent Highly Alienated
Most Alienated Groups	
Blacks	29%
Liberals	26%
High school education	25%
Skilled labor	25%
Western residents	25%
City residents	24%
Town residents	24%
Aged 30–49	24%
Least Alienated Groups	
White Catholics	21%
Conservatives	20%
Annual incomes under $7,000	20%
Aged 50 and over	19%
White Protestants	18%
Annual incomes $25,000 and over	18%
Southern residents	17%
Rural residents	16%
Professional occupation	16%

The findings from the survey show quite clearly that public concern with threats to individual privacy is related to level of alienation from technology and the institutions of government and business. Table P-3 shows that fully 47% of those who are highly alienated are "very concerned" about threats to their personal privacy and another 30% are "somewhat concerned." This percentage is 13 points above that for the total public and 21 points above those who are not alienated.

Table P-3   **Alienation and Concern with Threats to Privacy: Public**

Question   How concerned are you about threats to your personal privacy in America today? Would you say you're very concerned, somewhat concerned, only a little concerned, or not concerned at all?

		Alienation			
(Number of respondents)	Total Public (1,511)	High (315)	Moderate (424)	Low (511)	Not Alienated (261)
Very concerned	31%	47%	30%	27%	21%
Somewhat concerned	33%	30%	32%	33%	35%
Only a little concerned	17%	11%	20%	19%	17%
Not concerned at all	19%	12%	17%	21%	26%
Not sure	1%	*	*	1%	1%

Less than 0.5%

Professor Westin will utilize the alienation index in his analysis of the implications of these findings.

Privacy

The Surveys

The data for this project was collected in two separate surveys:

a. A survey of a nationwide cross-section of 1,513 adults interviewed between November 30 and December 10, 1978.

b. A survey of 11 leadership groups, involving interviews with business employers (200), executives in the credit (32), credit card (40), banking (36), insurance (36), and computer (36) industries, state insurance commissioners (33), congressmen and their aides (77), law enforcement officials (42), federal regulatory officials involved in enforcing privacy legislation (53), and doctors (33). All interviews were conducted between November 27, 1978 and January 4, 1979. This survey used a slightly different questionnaire from that used in the survey of the general public, but incorporated many of the same questions.

All interviews of the nationwide cross-section were conducted in person by Harris interviewers, under the control and supervision of the Harris Field Director and Regional Supervisors. All of the cross-section interviews were validated by telephone call-backs to ensure that the interviews had been honestly and accurately carried out.*

All interviews with the leadership groups were carried out by executive interviewers belonging to the Harris executive field force, under the control of the Executive Field Director.

The Sample Design

a. **The national cross-section:** The sample was designed to be representative of the adult civilian population of the continental United States, excluding Alaska and Hawaii, and those in prisons or hospitals. The sample design was based on updated census information on the population of each state, and on the population living in urbanized areas and in more rural areas throughout the country. The sample was stratified to ensure that it would reflect within 1 percentage point the actual proportion of those living in different regions, and in different size-of-place areas (city, suburb, town, rural). Within each stratum the selection of the ultimate sampling unit (a cluster of adjacent households) was achieved by multi-stage cluster sampling. Within each of sixteen strata (four regions within four size-of-place categories) first states, then counties, and then minor civil divisions and, where possible, census tracts and city blocks were selected proportional to census estimates of their respective populations.

Interviewers in the field were provided with detailed maps of the ultimate sampling units, and then they interviewed within the assigned respective areas. The national sample consisted of 200 such interviewing areas (sample points) throughout the country. At each sample point 1 respondent from each of 8 different households was interviewed. At each household the respondent was chosen by means of a random selection pattern geared to the number of adults of each sex living in that household. The representativeness of the sample is shown in the following table:

*Validation sheets listing the respondent name, address, and telephone number (if available) are sent to this office at the same time questionnaires are returned. Those respondents listed who do not have a telephone, or refused to provide a number, are sent a personal letter and return mail form asking five key questions from the study. The validation sheets are then sent to our telephone validation service where attempts are made to contact all listed names on three days at three different times of day. The same five key questions used on the mail validation form are asked by telephone. Those respondents who cannot be reached by telephone are then sent the personal letter and return mail form. If any doubt arises during validation about the authenticity of an interviewer's work, those interviews are dropped from the study.

	Number In Sample	Unweighted Percentage	Weighted Percentage
Total	**1,513**	**100**	**100**
Region			
East	434	29	28
Midwest	407	27	26
South	405	27	28
West	267	18	18
Size of Place			
Cities: central cities in urbanized areas (generally 50,000 or more)	488	32	33
Suburbs: urbanized areas outside central cities	430	28	28
Towns: other urban areas (generally 2,500 to 49,000)	231	15	15
Rural: anything not included above	364	24	24
Age			
18–29 years	424	28	30
30–49 years	563	37	33
50 and over	520	34	36
Education			
8th grade or less	136	9	10
Some high school, high school graduate	752	50	51
Some college, college graduate	615	41	39
Type of Work			
Professional	263	17	17
Executive	136	9	8
Proprietor	80	5	5
Skilled labor	336	22	21
White collar	298	20	20
Union member	410	27	26
Sex			
Male	762	50	48
Female	751	50	52
Income (total household income for 1978)			
Under $7,000	281	19	20
$7,000–$14,999	422	28	28
$15,000–$24,999	491	32	31
$25,000 and over	231	15	15

1. Subgroup totals do not always come to 1,513 because of some non-response.

2. East includes: Connecticut, Delaware, District of Columbia, Maine, Maryland, Massachusetts, New Hampshire, New Jersey, New York, Pennsylvania, Rhode Island, Vermont, and West Virginia.

   Midwest include: Illinois, Indiana, Iowa, Kansas, Michigan, Minnesota, Missouri, Nebraska, North Dakota, Ohio, South Dakota, and Wisconsin.

   South includes: Alabama, Arkansas, Florida, Georgia, Kentucky, Louisiana, Mississippi, North Carolina, Oklahoma, South Carolina, Tennessee, Texas, and Virginia.

   West includes: Arizona, California, Colorado, Idaho, Montana, Nevada, New Mexico, Oregon, Utah, Washington, and Wyoming.

b. **The leadership samples:** *Each of the six leadership samples were selected systematically from lists compiled from the following sources:*

Business Employers
Fortune listing of top 1000 companies.

Credit
Listing of top 300 savings banks, savings and loan associations, and Fortune listing top 50 financial companies.

Credit Card Companies
A list of the major credit card companies and the largest retailers and oil companies distributing credit cards.

Banks
A systematic sample of a list of the 300 largest commercial banks in the United States.

Insurance Companies
Fortune 1250.
Best's Insurance Reports.

Computer
Standard & Poor's Directory.

State Insurance Commissioners
A list of all state insurance commissioners.

Congress
A list of all congressmen serving on committees involved in privacy legislation.

Law Enforcement Officials
A list of all federal law enforcement agencies and the Senior Police Officers in the 200 largest cities.

Doctors
American Medical Association Directory.